PLANT PARA

LECTIN FREE DIET QUICK & EASY RECIPES TO FIGHT DISEASE AND CONTROL WEIGHT GAIN

Suzy Susson

FREE EBOOK DOWNLOAD

Download "Instant Pot Cookbook 1000" and other great cookbooks free

Simply go to https://recipesbysusson.blogspot.com/

DISCLAIMER/LEGAL NOTICE

TABLE OF CONTENT

INTRODUCTION
LECTINS. WHAT ARE THEY?

Lectins, which are universal in nature, are found in many foods, but mostly beans and grains. They are proteins found in high amounts in plants like whole grains, legumes, and some vegetables. In plants, lectins are mainly found in seeds, which happens to be the part most people love to eat. This kind of toxic protein is also found in small quantity in sour cream, eggs, milk, and some other dairy products.

LECTINS NEGATIVE EFFECTS ON THE BODY

Lectins have been known to have both positive and negative effects on health. These anti-nutrients usually bind carbohydrates together in the system, thereby preventing the absorption of some nutrients. They can cause digestion, chronic disease risk, and even cause red blood cells to band together.

If plant foods, like legumes, are eaten without being cooked, they may cause stomach upset. In raw or undercooked kidney beans, lectin can cause kidney bean poisoning in the form of severe nausea, diarrhea, and vomiting.

Other health problems that are caused by lectins include:

- Cavities
- Celiac disease
- Destroys digestive enzymes
- Digestive problems
- Increase the growth of pancreas
- Increases risk of developing autoimmune diseases
- Inflammatory bowel syndrome
- It causes an allergic reaction
- Leaky gut syndrome
- Nutritional deficiencies

Summarily, lectins that are found in large quantity in foods rich in carbohydrates will make it hard for the body to maintain its cells.

DEFINITION OF LECTIN-FREE DIET?

The lectin-free diet was popularized by Dr. Steven Gundry, a former heart surgeon who later switched to focusing on food and supplement-based medicine. He wrote a book titled The Plant Paradox Cookbook, in which he provides information on ways to avoid lectins, alternative food choices to lectin-rich foods, and a lot of healthy recipes. In his book, he emphasizes the need for people to choose to improve their health and also reduce their body weight at the same time.

The lectin-free diet completely avoids or limits foods that are high in lectin. Such foods include:

- Carbs
- Dairy Products
- Grains
- Pasta
- Quinoa
- Squash
- Uncooked Legumes
- Unpeeled and unseeded nightshade vegetables like peppers, potatoes, tomatoes, and eggplants

LECTIN-FREE FOODS TO EAT

The following foods are highly recommended by Dr. Gundry for people who need to limit the lectin in their diet.

- A2 Milk
- Asparagus
- Avocado
- Celery
- Cooked Sweet Potatoes
- Cruciferous Vegetables Like Brussels Sprouts And Broccoli
- Garlic And Onions
- Green And Leafy Vegetables
- Herbs Like Parsley, Basil, Mint, And Cilantro
- Mushrooms
- Olives Or Extra Virgin Olive Oil
- Pasture-Raised Meats

BENEFITS OF LECTIN-FREE DIET

It has been shown by studies conducted that low-lectin diet has a lot of health benefits. Some of these benefits are:

- Encourages the consumption of fresh vegetables and organic meat;
- Guarantees a brighter and clearer skin;
- Help you avoid highly toxic foods from your diet;
- Helps in combating diabetes;
- Helps in weight loss;
- Improves the quality of sleep;
- Increases energy levels;
- Reduces inflammation, consequently reducing the risk of depression, cancer, stroke, heart attack, and many cardiovascular diseases;
- Reduction of intestinal gas, belching, and bloating;

RISKS OF LECTIN-FREE DIET

Studies have shown that lectin, being a restrictive plan, may cut out or limit the intake of many nutritious foods like beans, whole grains, and some vegetables.

Below are some risks that come with going on a lectin-free diet:

- The consumption of whole grains can help in reducing the risk of heart diseases, cancer, obesity, and diabetes.
- Fruits and vegetables are very beneficial to health. They help to reduce the risk of heart and lung diseases, reduce the risk of cancer, and help in maintaining a healthy weight.
- Vegetarians and vegans will also find it hard to follow a lectin-free diet because it reduces consumption of plant foods that provide protein like legumes, seeds, nuts, and whole grains.
- Whole grains, legumes, fruits, and vegetable peels are very good sources of dietary fiber. Reduction in the intake of this fiber could cause constipation.
- A lectin-free diet is also quite expensive and hard to follow through the long-term.

HOW TO REDUCE LECTIN FROM FOODS AND EVERYDAY LIFE

Eliminating high-lectin foods completely from your diet can be really difficult. It is therefore recommended that dieters should avoid high-lectin foods whenever they can as they may not be able to do so all the time.

There are some ways to reduce the lectin content of the food we eat. Some of these ways include:

- Boiling
- Peeling
- Fermentation of vegetables
- Deseeding
- Sprouting
- Pressure cooking

Below are other ways of reducing lectin in your diet but still enjoy them occasionally:

- Pressure cook your meals using your Instant Pot. This is a healthier way to make your food healthier by retaining the nutrients and minerals in vegetables. The Instant Pot is perfect for eliminating plant lectins found in beans, tomatoes, legumes, potatoes, or quinoa. Pressure cooking does not touch the lectins in wheat, barley, oats. However, using the 'slow-cook' setting could increase lectin content.
- Peel and deseed fruits and veggies before eating them. If you must eat lectin-rich plant foods, be sure to peel and deseed them. Since lectins are mostly found in the peels and seeds of plants, try eliminating such parts.
- Choose white over brown. When you decide to eat grains, choose white grains over the brown ones. The hull of brown rice, for instance, contains a lot of dangerous lectins.

Since lectins have a lot of health benefits, it is not advisable to cut them off completely. The best way to go is to reduce their daily intake.

WHAT TO EAT WHEN ON A LECTIN-FREE DIET

The dietary restrictions of lectin-free diets are not as constraining as they may seem. There are so many delicious foods you can still enjoy that are lectin-free.

The recipes provided in this cookbook are made with lectin-free ingredients that are easy to adapt to. Once you can inculcate this new way of eating, you will be encouraged to stick to it long-term.

Here are some food items you can enjoy on a lectin-free lifestyle.

Grass-fed meat and pastured poultry:

- Bacon
- Beef
- Beef Liver
- Bison
- Bottom round roast
- Bratwursts
- Brisket
- Chicken
- Chicken drumsticks
- Chorizo
- Deer
- Duck
- Flank steak
- Goose
- Ground beef
- Ground lamb
- Ham
- Lamb
- Lamb's Leg
- Lamb's legs
- Lamb's Liver
- Lamb shank
- Lamb's shoulder
- Loin roast

- Pepperoni
- Pheasant
- Pot roast
- Quail
- Rabbit
- Ribeye steak
- Salami
- Sausage
- Short ribs
- Sirloin steak
- T-bone steak
- Turkey
- Turkey Legs
- Veal

Vegetables:

- Algae
- All cruciferous vegetables
- Artichokes
- Arugula
- Asparagus
- Basil
- Beets
- Bell peppers; peeled and de-seeded
- Bok choy
- Broccoli
- Brussel sprouts
- Cabbage; Napa, Chinese, purple, red cabbage, etc.
- Carrots
- Cauliflower
- Celery
- Chives
- Collards
- Cucumbers; peeled and de-seeded
- Fennel

- Garlic
- Kale
- Leeks
- Lettuce
- Mushrooms
- Mustard greens
- Okra
- Onions
- Parsley
- Pumpkin; seeds should be avoided
- Radishes
- Sauerkraut
- Scallions
- Sea vegetables
- Seaweed
- Spinach
- Sweet potatoes; in moderation
- Swiss chard
- Watercress

Nuts and seeds:

- Almonds
- Chestnuts
- Hemp seeds
- Macadamia nuts
- Pecans
- Pecans
- Pine nuts
- Pistachios
- Walnuts

Healthy oils and fats:

- Almond butter
- Avocado oil
- Coconut oil

- Ghee; clarified butter
- Olive oil

Wild-caught fish and seafood:

- Catfish
- Clams
- Crab
- Eels
- Fish fillets; tilapia, salmon, trout, cod, halibut, barramundi, etc.
- Lobster
- Mussels
- Octopus
- Oysters
- Scallops
- Shrimp

Other lectin-free foods:

- Nut flours; coconut, almond, arrowroot powder
- Nut milk, cream; coconut milk, almond milk, coconut cream, etc.
- Cacao powder
- Coconut aminos
- Coffee
- Dates
- Dark chocolate
- Mustard
- Natural sweeteners (Stevia, erythritol, monk fruit, swerve)
- Tahini sauce
- Dairy-free ice cream

WHAT TO AVOID WHEN ON A LECTIN-FREE DIET

To enjoy a lectin-free diet, one has to avoid lectins or restrict them from your diet. Here are some of the food items to avoid:

All grains:

- Barley
- Buckwheat
- Corn
- Cornmeal
- Flour
- Maize
- Millet
- Oats
- Pasta
- Quinoa
- Rice
- Rye
- Spelt
- Wheat

Refined starches:

- All bread
- Cereals
- Cookies

Flour; nut flours allowed

Pastries

Potatoes; (peeled sweet potatoes and peeled yams are allowed in moderation)

White Rice

All legumes:

- Black beans
- Boston beans

- Cashews
- Chickpeas
- Chili beans
- Fava beans
- Green beans
- Green peas
- Kidney beans
- Lentils
- Lima beans
- Mexican black beans
- Mexican red beans
- Peanuts
- Peanuts
- Pinto beans
- Pumpkin seeds; flesh and pureed pumpkin allowed
- Red beans
- Soybeans
- Sunflower seeds
- White beans

All dairy products:

- Butter
- Buttermilk
- Cheese; cheddar, mozzarella, swiss, parmesan, ricotta, cottage
- Coffee Creamer
- Heavy cream OR whipped cream
- Ice cream
- Ice milk
- Milk; whole, powdered, evaporated, chocolate
- Puddings
- Soy milk
- Yogurt

Sugar:

- Agave and aspartame

- All maple syrups
- All sugars
- Bee honey, store-bought honey

Fruits and vegetables:

- Bell peppers; if not peeled and de-seeded
- Cucumbers (IF NOT peeled and de-seeded)
- Eggplants
- Eggplants
- Goji berries, ground cherries, gooseberries, blueberries
- Melons
- Peas
- Potatoes
- Ripe bananas
- Squash
- Tomatillos
- Tomatoes; any tomato products, including ketchup
- Zucchini

FOOD SUBSTITUTES FOR LECTIN-FREE DIET

Not everything sold on our market shelves is healthy for us. There are a lot of really healthy foods you can take without missing your high-lectin foods. Here are some really healthy substitutions to keep you on a lectin-free diet:

- Substitute beans with: pressure-cooked beans, and pine nuts.
- Substitute cornstarch with: arrowroot powder or nut flour.
- Substitute dairy butter with: ghee; also called "clarified butter."
- Substitute diet soda with: infused sparkling water made with slices of lemon and orange, and sometimes fresh berries.
- Substitute pasta with: spiralized beets, carrots, sweet potatoes, and Daikon radish.
- Substitute peanut butter with: almond butter, walnut butter, hazelnut butter, Tahini (basically, sesame seed butter), and pistachio butter.
- Substitute regular barbeque sauce with: homemade, sugar-free barbecue sauce.
- Substitute rice with: millet, sorghum grain, and cauliflower rice
- Substitute soy sauce with: coconut aminos.
- Substitute sugar with: natural sweeteners, such as stevia.
- Substitute wheat flour with: almond flour, hazelnut flour, coconut flour, sesame flour.
- Substitute yogurt with: goat's milk yogurt, sheep milk's yogurt, buffalo's milk yogurt, coconut yogurt, and almond yogurt.

TIPS AND TRICKS FOR LECTIN-FREE DIETS

Going on a lectin-free diet involves limiting consumption of the following foods:

- Acorn squash and butternut squash.
- Beans, grains, and legumes.
- Cow Dairy.
- In-season fruits; in moderation.
- Nightshade vegetables, like peppers and tomatoes.
- Starchy potatoes, like sweet potatoes.

If you find it hard to avoid these food groups, try the following tips and tricks to guarantee success on a lectin-free diet:

- Make sure there is no high-lectin food in your refrigerator, food pantry, or kitchen as a whole. Such food, like sugar, all-purpose flour, and pasta should be gotten rid of to avoid temptations.
- Always have low-lectin snacks like fresh celery and baby carrots handy.
- Use sea salt, fresh herbs, black pepper, mustard, vinegar, fresh spices, and oils to enhance your meals if they taste bland.
- Ensure that your meals are minerals-rich, nutrients-rich, and vitamins-rich to ensure you each high-quality food.
- Do not patronize fast foods, deep fried foods, frozen meals, as well as processed meats and fish.
- Find and connect with other lectin-free dieters. Join their groups through social media and other places. Ask for advice when you need it.
- Try out new lectin-free recipes and create yours.
- Consult with your physician before you embark on a lectin-free diet. Be sure that a low-lectin diet will not affect your health negatively.

These tips and tricks are quite easy to follow and will grant you success on your lectin-free lifestyle.

LECTIN-FREE DIET INSTANT POT RECIPES
EGG AND BREAKFAST RECIPES

HARD BOILED EGG LOAF

Time: 10 minutes

Servings: 6

Ingredients:

12 large eggs

A pinch of salt

Pepper (to taste)

Instructions:

1. Pick a baking dish that fits into your Instant Pot. Then use a non-stick cooking spray to grease the dish.
2. Crack the large eggs into the baking dish. Use pepper and salt to season but do not stir.
3. Pour in a cup of water then place a steamer rack on the Instant Pot. Place the baking dish on top.
4. Close and seal the lid then set on Manual. Cook for 5 minutes on high pressure.
5. Naturally release the pressure for 5 minutes when it is done. Quick release any pressure left then take the lid off. Let the pan settle for 5 minutes.
6. Place the egg loaf on a cutting board and slice before serving.

Nutritional Information per Serving:

Carbohydrates: 0.3g

Dietary Fiber: 0g

Fat: 4.4g

Protein: 5.5g

Calories: 63

EGG HASH

Time: 30 minutes

Servings: 6

Ingredients:

¼ cup of fresh green onions (diced)

2 tablespoons of unsweetened almond milk or unsweetened coconut milk

4 medium-sized sweet potatoes (cubed)

8 chopped slices of bacon

12 large eggs (beaten)

A pinch of salt

Pepper (to taste)

Instructions:

1. Set the Instant Pot on Sauté mode then throw in the chopped bacon. Cool until it is browned then take it out of the pot and turn off 'Sauté'.
2. Grease a spring form pan and put the cooked bacon in it. Place the cubed potatoes on it.
3. Get a bowl and mix the eggs, milk, pepper and salt in it. Stir properly. Empty the contents of the bowl into the pan then use foil to cover it. Place the pan inside the Instant Pot.

4. Set on Manual and cook for 20 minutes on high pressure.
5. When it is done, release the pressure naturally and take off the lid.
6. Take out the pan and serve in plates. Garnish each plate with green onions before serving.

Nutrition Information per Serving:

Carbohydrates: 29.5g

Dietary Fiber: 4.3g

Fat: 20.7g

Protein: 22.2g

Calories: 394

SPINACH AND MUSHROOM FRITTATA

Time: 12 minutes

Servings: 4

Ingredients:

1 cup of water

1 cup of fresh baby spinach

6 slices of bacon (diced)

8 large eggs

A pinch of salt

Pepper (to taste)

Instructions:

1. Set the Instant Pot on Sauté mode then add the diced bacon. Cook until it is browned, then turn off the Sauté mode and set aside.
2. Get a large bowl then add the eggs, bacon, spinach, salt, and pepper to it. Stir properly.
3. Use nonstick cooking spray to grease 4 individual ramekins. Equally divide the egg mixture between the ramekins. Use aluminum foil to cover them.
4. Add a cup of water and place a trivet in the Instant Pot. Place the ramekins on the trivet.
5. Lock and seal the lid. Set the pot on Manual and cook for 5 minutes on high pressure.
6. Release the pressure naturally for 10 minutes when done. Take off the lid and serve.

Nutrition Information per Serving:

Carbohydrates: 3.2g

Dietary Fiber: 1.3g

Fat: 20.9g

Protein: 23.3g

Calories: 293

CAULIFLOWER PUDDING

Time: 30 minutes

Servings: 4

Ingredients:

1 cup of water

1 teaspoon of pure vanilla extract

1 cup of cauliflower rice (pulse florets in the food processor until it reaches rice-like consistency)

1 ½ cups of unsweetened almond milk or unsweetened coconut milk

2 teaspoons of organic ground cinnamon powder

Pinch of salt

Instructions:

1. Put all the ingredients in the Instant Pot and stir properly.
2. Set on Manual and cook for 20 minutes on high pressure.
3. Release the pressure naturally for 10 minutes after cooking. Quick release any pressure left then take off the lid.
4. Serve.

Nutrition Information per Serving:

Carbohydrates: 6.3g

Dietary Fiber: 2.5g

Fat: 21.6g

Protein: 22.2g

Calories: 213

COCONUT YOGURT WITH BERRIES

Time: 1 day

Servings: 32

Ingredients:

½ cup of unsweetened Greek yogurt

1 cup of Swerve or granulated Erythritol

2 cups of mixed berries

2 tablespoons of organic vanilla bean pasta

4 x 8-ouunces (1 gallon) of unsweetened coconut milk

Instructions:

1. Pour the coconut milk into the Instant Pot, then lock and seal the lid. Press 'Yogurt' and set on 'Boil'.
2. The Instant Pot will beep after about 45 minutes. Quick release the pressure and remove the lid. Let the coconut milk cool.
3. Stir in the Greek yogurt and vanilla bean pasta until properly combined.
4. Close and seal the lid, then set on 'Yogurt'. Adjust time to 8 hours.
5. Strain the yogurt into jars using cheese cloth then refrigerate overnight.
6. Clean the Instant Pot and set on Sauté mode. Simmer berries in it with granulated Erythritol.
7. Spoon the berry mixture over the yogurt and serve.

Nutrition Information per Serving:

Carbohydrates: 10.3g

Dietary Fiber: 0.9g

Fat: 6.9g

Protein: 1g

Calories: 73

CHORIZO WITH SWEET POTATO HASH

Time: 22 minutes

Servings: 6

Ingredients:

1 tablespoon of olive oil

1 pound of chorizo sausage (thinly sliced)

1 large white or yellow onion (finely chopped)

1 cup of homemade low-sodium vegetable broth

2 cloves of garlic (minced)

3 tablespoons of fresh rosemary

3 tablespoons of fresh basil (finely chopped)

4 bacon slices (chopped)

6 large sweet potatoes (cut into bite-sized pieces)

Pinch of salt

Pepper

Instructions:

1. Set the Instant Pot on Sauté and pour in the olive oil.
2. When it gets hot, add the garlic and onions then sauté while stirring occasionally until they soften.
3. Add the bacon, sweet potato cubes, and bacon.
4. Pour in the vegetable broth and sprinkle with pepper and salt.
5. Lock and seal the lid. Set the pot on Manual and cook for 10 minutes on high pressure.
6. When it is cooked, quick release the pressure and take off the lid.
7. If all the liquid does not evaporate, discard the remaining liquid.
8. Move to serving dishes then garnish with fresh rosemary and fresh basil. Serve.

Nutrition Information per Serving:

Carbohydrates: 43.4g

Dietary Fiber: 6.2g

Fat: 34.5g

Protein: 25.2g

Calories: 590

EGG AND ASPARAGUS FRITTATA

Time: 30 minutes

Servings: 4

Ingredients:

½ cup of unsweetened coconut milk or unsweetened almond milk

1 cup of fresh asparagus (stemmed and cut into bite-sized pieces)

2 tablespoons of fresh chives (chopped)

6 large eggs

Pinch of salt

Pepper

Instructions:

1. Use nonstick cooking spray to grease an 8-inch cake pan.
2. Get a bowl and mix the eggs, milk, salt, chives, asparagus, and pepper in it. Stir properly.
3. Pour the egg mixture into the cake pan and use foil to cover it.
4. Pour in a cup of water then place a trivet into the Instant Pot.
5. Place the cake pan on the trivet, then lock and seal the lid. Set the pot on Manual and cook for 23 minutes on high pressure.
6. Release the pressure naturally for 10 minutes when done, then quick release the remaining pressure.
7. Take off the lid and remove the pan. Let it set for 5 minutes before serving. Then serve.

Nutrition Information per Serving:

Carbohydrates: 3.4g

Dietary Fiber: 1.4g

Fat: 13.8g

Protein: 9.7g

Calories: 170

SAUSAGE AND CAULIFLOWER MASH

Time: 12 minutes

Servings: 2

Ingredients:

½ cup vegetable broth

½ cup of unsweetened almond milk or unsweetened coconut milk

1 tablespoon of arrowroot powder

1 teaspoon of organic mustard powder

1 large head cauliflower (cut into florets)

1 tablespoon of non-dairy butter or ghee (melted)

1½ cups of water

2 tablespoons of olive oil

2 cups of ground sausage (mild or spicy)

Pinch of sea salt

Pepper

Instructions:

1. Pour a cup of water into the Instant Pot and place a trivet inside. Place a cauliflower on the trivet.
2. Lock the lid and seal the valve. Set on Manual and cook for 4 minutes on high pressure.
3. Quick release the pressure and take off the lid. Remove the cauliflower and trivet and throw away the water. Place the cauliflower in a dish that is ovenproof and let it warm at 200oF.

4. Get a large bowl and put the cauliflower, ghee, milk, mustard powder, pepper, and salt in it. Mash the cauliflower with a potato masher until it breaks aside, then set it aside.
5. Set the Instant Pot on Sauté mode and heat the olive oil in it. Add the ground sausage until it browns.
6. Add vegetable broth and ½ cup of water to the Pot and stir.
7. Close and seal the lid then set the Instant Pot on Manual. Cook for 8 minutes on high pressure.
8. Quick release the pressure when done, then remove the lid.
9. Set the Instant Pot on sauté mode again, and sprinkle the arrowroot flour on the ingredients. Stir occasionally until it thickens.
10. Place the cauliflower rice in serving dishes then spoon the sausage and sauce on the cauliflower. Then serve.

Nutrition Information per Serving:

Carbohydrates: 31.2g

Dietary Fiber: 11.8g

Fat: 47.2g

Protein: 17.3g

Calories: 618

TURKEY SAUSAGE FRITTATA

Time: 28 minutes

Servings: 4

Ingredients:

1 teaspoon of salt

1 tablespoon of olive oil

1 teaspoon of freshly cracked black pepper

1 cup of unsweetened almond milk or unsweetened coconut milk

1½ cups of ground turkey breakfast sausage

12 large eggs (beaten)

Instructions:

1. Set the Instant Pot on sauté mode then pour in the olive oil.
2. Add the breakfast turkey and cook while stirring occasionally until it turns brown. Turn the sauté mode off and set aside.
3. Use nonstick cooking spray to grease a spring form pan then place the cooked turkey in the pan.
4. Get a bowl and mix the eggs, milk, pepper, and salt in it and stir properly. Pour the mixture on the turkey.
5. Pour 2 cups of water into the Instant Pot and place a trivet in it.
6. Place the spring form pan on the trivet.
7. Lock the lid and seal the valve. Set the Instant Pot on Manual and cook for 7 minutes on High pressure.
8. After cooking, release the pressure naturally and take off the lid.
9. Take off the pan and leave to settle for 5 minutes before slicing. Then serve.

Nutrition Information per Serving:

Carbohydrates: 4.3g

Dietary Fiber: 1.3g

Fat: 31.7g

Protein: 42.9g

Calories: 471

BROCCOLI HAM FRITTATA

Time: 40 minutes

Servings: 4

Ingredients:

¼ cup of organic ham (cubed)

1 cup of unsweetened almond milk or coconut milk

2 cups of fresh broccoli florets (chopped small pieces)

4 eggs

Pepper

Pinch of salt

Instructions:

1. Get a baking pan that fits into your Instant Pot and use a nonstick cooking spray to grease it.
2. Get a bowl then put the broccoli pieces and cubed ham in it. Stir properly to combine.
3. Spread the mixture from the bowl on the bottom of the pan in a single layer.
4. Get a bowl and whisk the eggs, milk, pepper and salt in it.
5. Pour the egg mixture over the broccoli and ham.
6. Pour two cups of water into the Instant Pot and place a steamer rack in it.
7. Place the baking pan on the steamer rack, then close and seal the lid.
8. Set on Manual and cook on high pressure for 20 minutes.
9. After cooking, release the pressure naturally and take off the lid.
10. Remove the pan and let it settle for 5 minutes before you slice. Serve.

Nutrition Information per Serving:

Carbohydrates: 8.92g

Dietary Fiber: 1.83g

Fat: 16.3g

Protein: 27.43g

Calories: 423

SOUPS AND STEWS RECIPES

MINESTRONE SOUP WITH ITALIAN SAUSAGE

Time: 28 minutes

Servings: 8

Ingredients:

1 cup of mushrooms (sliced)

1 pound of ground Hot Italian sausage

1 tablespoon of low-sodium coconut aminos

1 medium-sized yellow onion (finely chopped)

1 medium-sized orange carrot (finely chopped)

2 tablespoons of olive oil

2 cups of fresh broccoli florets

2 cups of fresh cauliflower florets

2 tablespoons of fresh parsley (finely chopped)

4 cups of baby spinach

4 cloves of garlic (minced)

6 cups of homemade organic low-sodium chicken broth

Pinch of salt

Pepper

Instructions:

1. Set the Instant Pot on Sauté mode then pour in the olive oil. When it gets hot, add the ground sausage. Keep stirring while cooking, until it is no longer pink.
2. Add the carrots, mushrooms, onion, and garlic. Then cook for additional 2 to 4 minutes, until they soften.
3. Stir in the cauliflower, broccoli, and chicken broth.
4. Lock and seal the lid. Set the Instant Pot on annual and cook for 8 minutes on high pressure.
5. Release the pressure naturally for 5 minutes when done, then quick release the remaining pressure. Take off the lid.
6. Add the coconut aminos, baby spinach, pepper, and salt. Stir while heating, until the spinach wilts.
7. Scoop into bowls and serve.

Nutrition Information per Serving:

Carbohydrates: 12.02g

Dietary Fiber: 1.2g

Fat: 51.35g

Protein: 26.39g

Calories: 486

ROASTED GARLIC SOUP

Time: 35 minutes

Servings: 6

Ingredients:

¼ cup of ghee or non-dairy butter

1 cup of unsweetened coconut cream

1 large cauliflower head (finely chopped)

2 bulbs of garlic (about 20 garlic cloves)

3 medium shallots or onions (finely chopped)

6 cups of homemade low-sodium vegetable broth

Pinch of salt

Pepper

Instructions:

1. Set the Instant Pot on Sauté mode and place the ghee inside.
2. When it gets hot, add the garlic and onions, then sauté for additional 3 to 5 minutes.
3. Add the cauliflower and vegetable broth. Season with salt and black pepper to taste.
4. Close and seal the lid. Set on Manual and cook for 30 minutes on high pressure.
5. When cooked, quick release the pressure and take off the lid.
6. Puree the soup with an immersion blender until it is smooth.
7. Stir the coconut cream in.
8. Ladle into bowls and serve.

Nutrition Information per Serving:

Carbohydrates: 8.17g

Dietary Fiber: 2g

Fat: 14.05g

Protein: 2.94g

Calories: 156

CHICKEN TURMERIC SOUP

Time: 30 minutes

Servings: 4

Ingredients:

½ cup of unsweetened coconut cream

1 bay leaf

1 cup of broccoli florets

1 cup of cauliflower florets

1 teaspoon of cumin powder

1 yellow onion (finely chopped)

1 cup of carrots (finely chopped)

1 teaspoon of fresh ginger (grated)

1 cup of celery stalks (finely chopped)

1½ pounds boneless, skinless chicken breasts or chicken thighs

2 garlic cloves (minced)

2 tablespoons of ghee, olive oil, or coconut oil

2 cups of swiss chard (stemmed and roughly chopped)

3 teaspoons of turmeric powder

4 cups of organic homemade low-sodium vegetable or chicken broth or bone

Pepper

Pinch of salt

Pinch of cayenne pepper

Fresh cilantro (lemon wedges)

Instructions:

1. Set the Instant Pot on Sauté mode and pour in the olive oil.
2. Add the chicken as soon as it gets hot and sear each side for about 2 minutes until it is browned. Remove it and set aside.
3. Place the onion, garlic, and ginger in the Instant Pot. Sauté until they all soften.
4. Throw in the cauliflower, carrots, broccoli, and celery then sauté for an additional minute. Put the chicken back into the pot. Then add broth, turmeric powder, cayenne pepper, bay leaf, cumin powder, pepper, and salt. Stir properly.
5. Lock and seal the lid. Set the pot on Manual and cook for 8 minutes on high pressure.
6. After cooking, release the pressure naturally for 5 minutes. Take off the lid. Take out the bay leaf.
7. Pour in the coconut cream and swiss chard. Stir until chard wilts.
8. Scoop the soup into bowls. Use lemon wedges and fresh cilantro to garnish before serving.

Nutrition Information per Serving:

Carbohydrates: 11.71g

Dietary Fiber: 3.4g

Fat: 42.65g

Protein: 42.53g

Calories: 428

LEAK AND CAULIFLOWER SOUP

Time: 19 minutes

Servings: 8

Ingredients:

⅓ cup of fresh cilantro (finely chopped)

½ teaspoon of fresh nutmeg

½ cup of unsweetened coconut cream

1 pound of leeks (chopped)

1 bay leaf

1 large head of cauliflower (chopped into florets)

2 carrots (chopped)

2 celery stalks (finely chopped)

3 tablespoons of olive oil

4 garlic cloves (minced)

8 cups of homemade organic low-sodium chicken or vegetable broth

Pepper

Pinch of salt,

Instructions:

1. Set the Instant Pot on Sauté mode and pour in the oil.

2. When it gets hot, add the celery, garlic, cauliflower, and leeks. Sauté until the leeks wilt.
3. Add the nutmeg, pepper, salt, and broth. Stir properly.
4. Lock and seal the lid. Set on Manual and cook for 8 minutes on high pressure.
5. Afterwards, release the pressure naturally then take off the leaf. Remove the bay leaf from the pot.
6. Pulse the ingredients inside your Instant Pot with an immersion blender until they reach desired smoothness.
7. Stir in the fresh cilantro and unsweetened coconut cream. Season to taste and serve.

Nutrition Information per Serving:

Carbohydrates: 13.75g

Dietary Fiber: 1.2g

Fat: 10.63g

Protein: 2.69g

Calories: 151

CHICKEN LIME AVOCADO SOUP

Time: 18 minutes

Servings: 4

Ingredients:

½ cup of fresh cilantro (finely chopped)

1 teaspoon of ground cumin

1½ cups of fresh green onions (finely chopped)

2 garlic cloves (minced)

2 medium-sized carrots (finely chopped)

2 tablespoons of avocado oil, olive oil, or coconut oil

2 pounds of boneless, skinless chicken breasts or chicken thighs

3 fresh celery stalks (finely chopped)

4 medium-sized avocados (peeled, cored, finely chopped)

8 cups of homemade low-sodium chicken broth

Pepper

Pinch of salt

Juice and zest from 2 limes

Instructions:

1. Set the Instant Pot on sauté mode then heat the oil in it.
2. Sear each side of the chicken in the hot oil for about 2 minutes until uniformly browned.
3. Add the garlic, chicken broth, green onions, carrots, lime juice, celery, and lime zest.
4. Close and seal the lid. Set the pot on Manual and cook for 8 minutes on high pressure.
5. When done, release the pressure naturally then carefully take off the lid.
6. Place the chicken on a cutting board and use 2 forks to shred it. Place the shredded chicken in the Instant Pot.
7. Use pepper, salt, and cumin to season the chicken.
8. Use chopped avocados and fresh cilantro as toppings.
9. Serve

Nutrition Information per Serving:

Carbohydrates: 16.3g

Dietary Fiber: 6.83g

Fat: 22.4g

Protein: 33.2g

Calories: 402

HAMBURGER VEGETABLE SOUP

Time: 19 minutes

Servings: 10

Ingredients:

1 large sweet potato (peeled and cubed)

1 teaspoon of cider vinegar

1 teaspoon of Stevia

1 cup of pureed pumpkin

1 medium-sized red onion (finely chopped)

1 pound of extra lean grass-fed ground beef

2 tablespoons of olive oil

2 cups of fresh red cabbage (shredded)

2 cups of fresh green cabbage (shredded)

4 garlic cloves (minced)

3 fresh celery ribs (finely chopped)

3 fresh orange carrots (peeled and finely chopped)

4 cups of homemade low-sodium chicken broth

Pepper

Pinch of salt

Instructions:

1. Set the Instant Pot on sauté mode and heat the oil in it.
2. Throw in the onions and garlic then sauté for 2 minutes until they soften.
3. Add the ground beef and cook until it is no longer pink.
4. Throw in the celery, cubed sweet potatoes, and carrots. Cook for an additional minute.
5. Stir in the chicken broth, pureed pumpkin, red cabbage, green cabbage, Stevia, cider vinegar, black pepper, and salt.
6. Lock and seal the lid. Set on Manual then cook for 9 minutes on high pressure.
7. Afterwards, release the pressure naturally for 5 minutes. Quick release the remaining pressure and take off the lid.
8. Stir the soup and season to taste.
9. Ladle into bowls and serve.

Nutrition Information per Serving:

Carbohydrates: 7.3g

Dietary Fiber: 3.9g

Fat: 5.3g

Protein: 14.3g

Calories: 132

THAI BROCCOLI AND BEEF SOUP

Time: 20 minutes

Servings: 4

Ingredients:

⅓ cup of fresh cilantro (finely chopped)

1 teaspoon of organic fish sauce

1 2-inch ginger (peeled and minced)

1 cup of unsweetened coconut cream

1 pound of lean, grass-fed ground beef

2 large heads of broccoli (chopped into florets)

2 tablespoons of organic Thai green curry paste

2 tablespoons of olive oil

1 medium-sized onion (finely chopped)

2 garlic cloves (minced)

3 tablespoons of low-sodium coconut aminos

4 cups of homemade low-sodium chicken or beef broth

Pinch of salt

Pepper

Instructions:

1. Set your Instant Pot on Sauté mode and heat the olive oil in it.
2. When it gets hot, add the onions and sauté for 2 to 4 minutes.
3. Then add the ginger, green curry paste, and garlic. Cook for 1 minute.

4. Add the ground beef and cook until it is no longer pink.
5. Stir in the fish sauce, coconut aminos, pepper and salt. Afterwards, add the broth.
6. Close and seal the lid. Set on Manual and cook for 8 minutes on high pressure.
7. When cooked, release the pressure naturally for 5 minutes. Take the lid off carefully.
8. Stir in the broccoli florets and allow them heat through for a few minutes.
9. Stir in the coconut cream and season to taste. Scoop into bowls and serve.

Nutrition Information per Serving:

Carbohydrates: 5.6g

Dietary Fiber: 2.9g

Fat: 34.33g

Protein: 27.35g

Calories: 422

CHICKEN KALE SOUP

Time: 35 minutes

Servings: 6

Ingredients:

¼ cup of lemon juice

½ cup of coconut oil, avocado oil, olive oil, or ghee

1 teaspoon of lemon zest

1 yellow onion (finely chopped)

1 teaspoon of smoked paprika or regular paprika

1 large bunch of kale (stemmed and roughly chopped)

2 garlic cloves (minced)

2 tablespoons of organic taco seasoning

2 pounds of boneless, skinless chicken breasts or chicken thighs

4 cups of homemade low-sodium chicken broth

Pepper

Pinch of salt

Fresh green onions (diced)

Instructions:

1. Sauté the Instant Pot and pour in 1 tablespoon of olive oil.
2. When it gets hot, add the chicken and sear each side for 2 minutes until they are browned.
3. Put the chicken broth, garlic, onion, and olive oil remaining into a blender. Blend until very smooth then pour into the Instant Pot.
4. Stir in the lemon juice, kale, lemon zest, taco seasoning, salt, paprika, and pepper.
5. Lock and seal the lid. Set on Manual and cook for 10 minutes on high pressure.
6. When cooked, release the pressure naturally for 10 minutes, then quick release the remaining pressure.
7. Scoop into bowls and use fresh green onion to garnish. Serve.

Nutrition Information per Serving:

Carbohydrates: 2.4g

Dietary Fiber: 1.1g

Fat: 22.32g

Protein: 15.3g

Calories: 273

SPINACH SHIITAKE MUSHROOM SOUP

Time: 15 minutes

Servings: 6

Ingredients:

¼ cup of fresh parsley (finely chopped)

1 bay leaf

1 teaspoon of dried thyme

1 fresh lemon (juice and zest)

1 yellow onion (finely chopped)

1 cup of unsweetened coconut cream

1 pound of fresh green asparagus (trimmed and cut into 1-inch pieces)

2 tablespoons of olive oil or ghee

2 cups of fresh shiitake mushrooms (thinly sliced)

4 garlic cloves (minced)

4 cups of fresh baby spinach (roughly chopped)

4 cups of homemade low-sodium vegetable or chicken broth

Pinch of salt

Pepper

Instructions:

1. Set the Instant Pot on sauté mode and pour in the oil.
2. When it gets hot, add the onions and garlic. Stir occasionally while you sauté for 1 minute.
3. Add the mushrooms and pieces of asparagus then sauté for 2 to 4 minutes.
4. Stir in the vegetable broth, bay leaf, baby spinach, parsley, dried thyme, lemon zest, lemon juice, black pepper, and salt.
5. Lock and seal the lid. Set on Manual and cook for 9 minutes on high pressure.
6. Afterwards, release the pressure naturally then take off the lid. Take the bay leaf out.
7. Stir the unsweetened coconut cream in. Season to taste. Serve.

Nutrition Information per Serving:

Carbohydrates: 10.75g

Dietary Fiber: 3.8g

Fat: 8.53g

Protein: 8.54g

Calories: 237

ZUPPA TOSCANA

Time: 28 minutes

Servings: 10

Ingredients:

1 teaspoon of dried oregano

1 large yellow onion (finely chopped)

1 large bunch kale (stemmed and chopped)

1½ cups of unsweetened coconut cream or non-dairy cream

2 pounds of ground hot Italian sausage

4 slices of bacon

4 garlic cloves (minced)

6 cups of cauliflower florets (finely chopped)

6 cups of homemade low-sodium chicken broth

Pinch of salt

Pepper

Instructions:

1. Sauté the Instant Pot and place the bacon in it to cook until it browns. Set it aside.
2. Place the ground sausage in the Instant Pot and cook until it isn't pink anymore.
3. Add the cloves of garlic and onions, then sauté for few minutes.
4. Throw in the cauliflower florets, dried oregano, chicken broth, pepper, and salt. Stir to mix.
5. Lock and seal the lid. Set on Manual and cook for 5 minutes on high pressure.
6. When cooked, release the pressure naturally for 10 minutes. Take off the lid.
7. Stir in the kale until the heat from the ingredients heat it.
8. Pour in the coconut cream and stir. Use pepper and salt to season to taste. Serve.

Nutrition Information per Serving:

Carbohydrates: 17.69g

Dietary Fiber: 5.1g

Fat: 43.26g

Protein: 52.24g

Calories: 646

CHICKEN RECIPES

CHICKEN CHILI

Time: 28 minutes

Servings: 6

Ingredients:

½ teaspoon of organic ground cinnamon

1 cup of vegetable broth

1 small can of diced tomatoes

1 small can of red kidney beans

1 small can of organic tomato puree

1 tablespoon of organic ground cumin

1 medium yellow onion (finely chopped)

2 pounds of ground chicken

2 tablespoons of taco seasoning

2 tablespoons of organic chili powder

2 cups of homemade low-sodium chicken broth

3 tablespoons of olive oil

3 fresh celery stalks (finely chopped)

4 garlic cloves (minced)

Pinch of salt, pepper

Juice from 1 fresh lime

For serving: fresh cilantro, avocado slices

Instructions:

1. Set the Instant Pot on Sauté mode and pour in the olive oil.
2. When it gets hot, add the celery and onion then cook for 3 minutes before adding the garlic. Cook for additional 2 minutes.
3. Add the ground chicken and cook until it is not pink anymore.
4. While stirring, add the chili powder, cumin, taco seasoning, cinnamon, pepper, and salt.
5. While stirring, also add the tomato puree, kidney beans, diced tomatoes, vegetable broth, and lime juice.
6. Close and seal the lid. Set on Manual and cook for 12 minutes on high pressure.
7. When it is cooked, release the pressure naturally for 10 minutes. Quick release the remaining pressure. Take off the lid.
8. Scoop into bowls. Use slices of avocado and fresh cilantro to garnish. Then serve.

Nutrition Information per Serving:

Carbohydrates: 22.4g

Dietary Fiber: 3.3g

Fat: 12.2g

Protein: 47.2g

Calories: 395

FAUX-TISSERIE WHOLE CHICKEN

Time: 45 minutes

Servings: 8

Ingredients:

1 lemon (quartered)

1 tablespoon of dried basil

1 x 3-pound whole chicken

1 tablespoon of chili powder

1 tablespoon of onion powder

1 teaspoon of organic ground cumin

1 cup of homemade low-sodium chicken broth

2 tablespoons of fresh thyme (finely chopped)

2 tablespoons of fresh marjoram (finely chopped)

4 tablespoons of olive oil

6 cloves of garlic (minced)

Pinch of salt

Pepper

Instructions:

1. Drizzle a little layer of oil on the chicken.
2. Get a bowl, and mix the marjoram, basil, onion powder, thyme, chili powder, ground cumin, black pepper, and salt in it. Set the bowl aside.
3. Stuff the lemon and garlic inside the chicken then use a string to secure the chicken legs.
4. Set the Instant Pot on Sauté mode then when it gets hot, place the chicken in it. Sear all the sides of the chicken.
5. Sprinkle the chicken skin with seasoning.

6. Add the chicken broth to the Instant Pot and place a trivet inside. Drop the chicken on the trivet.
7. Close and seal the lid. Set on Manual and cook for 25 minutes on high pressure.
8. After cooking, release the pressure naturally for 15 minutes. Quick release the remaining pressure and take off the lid. Place the chicken on a platter and leave it there to rest for 10 minutes. Take out the lemon and garlic then slice.
9. Serve with salad on the side.

Nutrition Information per Serving:

Carbohydrates: 4.3g

Dietary Fiber: 0.9g

Fat: 33.2g

Protein: 34g

Calories: 483

BARBECUE CHICKEN SLIDERS

Time: 25 minutes

Servings: 4

Chicken Sliders:

4 boneless, skinless chicken breasts

Lettuce leaves – your choice, for buns

Barbecue Sauce:

¼ cup of Swerve sweetener

¼ cup of apple cider vinegar

⅓ cup of Worcestershire sauce

½ cup of coconut butter or ghee (clarified butter)

1 large yellow onion (finely chopped)

1 apple (peeled, cored, and finely chopped)

1 tablespoon of organic cayenne pepper

2 tablespoons of organic chili powder

3 tablespoons of organic brown mustard

3 cups of fresh cherries (pitted and halved)

6 cloves of garlic (minced)

Instructions:

1. Put all the ingredients for the barbecue sauce together in a blender. Pulse until it becomes very smooth.
2. Sauté your Instant Pot and pour in the olive oil. When hot, cook the onion and garlic in the oil for 3 minutes.
3. Put the chicken breasts into the pot and pour over the barbecue sauce.
4. Close and seal the lid. Set on Manual and cook for 15 minutes on high pressure.
5. When it is cooked, either naturally release or quick release the pressure. Take off the lid carefully.
6. Place the chicken on a cutting board, then use 2 forks to shred it.
7. Put the shredded chicken in the Instant Pot and stir properly to coat.
8. Scoop out the chicken and place them on lettuce leaves. Then serve.

Nutrition Information per Serving:

Carbohydrates: 27.54g

Dietary Fiber: 4.3g

Fat: 50.54g

Protein: 63.32g

Calories: 820

ITALIAN DRUMSTICKS

Time: 29 minutes

Servings: 8

Ingredients:

⅔ cup of homemade low-sodium chicken broth

1 teaspoon of chili powder

1 medium beet (finely chopped)

1 tablespoon of Italian seasoning

1 pound of fresh orange carrots (finely chopped)

1 teaspoon of smoked or regular paprika

1 medium-sized red or yellow onion (finely chopped)

2 tablespoons of olive oil

2 tablespoons of lemon juice

2 tablespoons of balsamic vinegar

3 tablespoons of dried thyme

8 cloves of garlic (minced)

8 skin-on chicken drumsticks

Pinch of salt

Pepper

Marinara Sauce:

1 medium beet (finely chopped)

1 pound of fresh orange carrots (finely chopped)

⅔ cup of homemade low-sodium chicken broth

2 tablespoons of lemon juice

Instructions:

1. Use pepper and salt to season the drumsticks.
2. Put the beets, chicken broth, carrots, and lemon juice together in a food processor or blender. Pulse until it becomes smooth.
3. Set the Instant Pot on Sauté mode, then pour in the olive oil.
4. Add onions when the oil gets hot, then sauté for 3 minutes. Add the garlic and sauté for 1 minute. Turn the sauté mode off.
5. Put the drumsticks inside the Instant Pot. Add the marinara sauce, paprika, chili powder, balsamic vinegar, Italian seasoning, and thyme to the pot.
6. Close and seal the lid. Set on Manual and cook for 15 minutes on high pressure.
7. When it is done, release the pressure naturally for 5 minutes, before quick releasing the remaining pressure. Take the lid off.
8. Place on a platter then use fresh basil to garnish. Serve.

Nutrition Information per Serving:

Carbohydrates: 6.89g

Dietary Fiber: 1.8g

Fat: 16.85g

Protein: 28.5g

Calories: 300

LEMON CHICKEN

Time: 19 minutes

Servings: 6

Ingredients:

½ cup of homemade low-sodium chicken broth

1 lemon (thinly sliced)

1 teaspoon of organic garlic powder

1 small yellow onion (finely chopped)

1 tablespoon of fresh parsley (finely chopped)

1 teaspoon of organic smoked or regular paprika

2 tablespoons of ghee (clarified butter)

2 tablespoons of organic Italian seasoning

3 tablespoons of olive oil

4 cloves of garlic (minced)

6 boneless, skinless chicken thighs or chicken breasts

Zest and juice from 1 lemon

Pinch of salt

Pepper

Instructions:

1. Get a bowl and put the garlic powder, pepper, salt, paprika, and Italian seasoning inside. Use the mixture to coat all the sides of the chicken.
2. Set the Instant Pot on Sauté mode and pour in the olive oil.
3. When it gets hot, stir infrequently while cooking the onions and garlic for 2 minutes. Add the chicken and sear on its sides. Then stir in the ghee, lemon zest, and lemon juice.
4. Arrange the lemon slices on the chicken.
5. Lock and seal the lid. Set on Manual and cook for 8 minutes on high pressure.
6. After it gets done, release the pressure naturally for 5 minutes. Quick release the remaining pressure and take off the lid.
7. Place on a platter. Then use fresh parsley and fresh lemon slices to garnish it. Serve.

Nutrition Information per Serving:

Carbohydrates: 1.8g

Dietary Fiber: 0.5g

Fat: 22.1g

Protein: 42.5g

Calories: 380

GARLIC AND SMOKED PAPRIKA DRUMSTICKS

Time: 35 minutes

Servings: 10

Ingredients:

1 cup of water

2 tablespoons of garlic powder

2 tablespoons of smoked paprika

10 fresh chicken drumsticks or chicken legs

Olive oil

Pepper

Pinch of salt

Instructions:

1. Mix the garlic powder, smoked paprika, pepper, and salt together in a bowl. Stir to combine.
2. Drizzle very little oil over the chicken then use the spice mixture to season the legs or drumsticks.
3. Pour a cup of water into the Instant Pot. Place the trivet in the pot.
4. Keep the drumsticks on the trivet.
5. Lock and seal the lid. Set on Manual and cook for 16 minutes on high pressure.
6. When cooked, release the pressure naturally for 5 minutes, and quick release the remaining pressure. Take off the lid then remove the chicken and place it on a baking sheet lined with parchment.
7. Put the baking tray under broiler, 2 minutes for each side, until each side of the skin become crispy with a golden color.
8. Move to a platter and serve.

Nutrition Information per Serving:

Carbohydrates: 3.2g

Dietary Fiber: 0.3g

Fat: 32g

Protein: 33.4g

Calories: 473

CHICKEN CARNITAS

Time: 40 minutes

Servings: 6

Ingredients:

¼ cup of homemade low-sodium chicken broth

1 bay leaf

1 fresh lime (juice)

1 teaspoon of chili powder

1 teaspoon of dried oregano

1 yellow onion (finely chopped)

1 tablespoon of organic ground cumin

2 tablespoons of olive oil

2 pounds of boneless, skinless chicken breasts or chicken thighs

5 cloves of garlic (minced)

Fresh cilantro (finely chopped)

Juice and zest from 1 fresh orange

Pepper

Pinch of salt

Dressing:

½ cup of homemade mayonnaise; lectin-free compliant ingredients

1 tablespoon of non-dairy milk; unsweetened coconut milk or unsweetened almond

Pinch of sea salt

Pinch of garlic powder

To serve: Fresh cilantro, tortilla shells, and purple onion

Instructions:

1. Put the ingredients for dressing together in a bowl. Mix and set aside.
2. Mix the cumin, oregano, chili powder, pepper, and salt in another bowl. Use it in seasoning the chicken.
3. Set the Instant Pot on Sauté mode then pour in the olive oil. When it gets hot, add the garlic and onions then cook for 3 minutes. Add chicken and sear all its sides.
4. Pour in the orange juice, lime juice, orange zest, chicken broth, cilantro, and bay leaf.
5. Close and seal the lid. Set on Manual and cook for 9 minutes on high pressure.
6. Release the pressure naturally when done. Take off the lid and remove the bay leaf.
7. Move the chicken to a cutting board then use 2 forks to shred it. Move it to a baking sheet then drizzle the cooking liquid on it. Place in oven to broil for 10 minutes, let it be turned halfway.
8. Scoop the chicken onto the tortilla shells. Use the fresh cilantro and purple onion to dress it. Serve.

Nutrition Information per Serving:

Carbohydrates: 6.21g

Dietary Fiber: 0.9g

Fat: 7.2g

Protein: 27.3g

Calories: 203

CHICKEN PAPRIKASH

Time: 25 minutes

Servings: 4

Ingredients:

1 bay leaf

1 cup of unsweetened coconut cream

1 large yellow onion (finely chopped)

1½ cups homemade low-sodium chicken broth

2 cloves of garlic (minced)

2 pounds bone-in, skinless, chicken breasts or chicken thighs

3 tablespoons of paprika

3 tablespoons of coconut oil or olive oil

5 tablespoons of arrowroot powder

Juice and zest from 1 fresh lemon

Pepper

Pinch of salt

Instructions:

1. Use pepper and salt to season the chicken.
2. Set the Instant Pot on Sauté mode and pour in the olive oil to heat.
3. When it gets hot, put in the garlic and onions then sauté for 3 minutes.
4. Add the chicken and sear all its sides until they are evenly browned.
5. Stir in the paprika, chicken broth, black pepper, lemon juice, lemon zest, bay leaf, and salt.
6. Close and seal the lid. Set on Manual and cook for 7 minutes on high pressure.
7. When it is done, release the pressure naturally for 10 minutes, then quick release any pressure left. Take off the lid, then remove the bay leaf.
8. Set on Sauté mode. Add the arrowroot powder and stir to coat the ingredients. Pour in the coconut cream then let it simmer until the sauce gets thicker. Season to taste.
9. Move to a platter then use fresh parsley to garnish it. Serve.

Nutrition Information per Serving:

Carbohydrates: 14.2g

Dietary Fiber: 1.7g

Fat: 43.31g

Protein: 67g

Calories: 720

GARLIC DRUMSTICKS

Time: 25 minutes

Servings: 6

Ingredients:

¼ cup of homemade low-sodium chicken broth

½ cup of low-sodium coconut aminos

½ onion (finely chopped)

1 teaspoon of olive oil

1 1-inch fresh ginger (peeled, then minced)

2 tablespoons of stevia

2 cloves of garlic (minced)

2 tablespoons of cider vinegar

6 skin-on fresh chicken drumsticks

Pepper

Pinch of salt

Instructions:

1. Use pepper and salt to season the drumsticks.
2. Set the Instant Pot on Sauté Mode, then pour in the olive oil.
3. When it heats, add the garlic and onion. Cook for 2 minutes before adding the drumsticks to the pot. Sear the drumsticks.
4. Stir in the chicken broth, ginger, stevia, cider vinegar, and coconut aminos.
5. Lock and seal the lid. Set on Manual then cook for 9 minutes on high pressure.

6. When it is done, release the pressure naturally for 5 minutes, then quick release the remaining pressure. Take off the lid.
7. Place the drumsticks on a baking pan lined with parchment. Place in oven to broil, 2 minutes for each side.
8. Set the Instant Pot on Sauté mode. Let the liquid simmer until it reduces halfway.
9. Move the drumsticks to a platter then pour the sauce on it. Use parsley to garnish. Then serve.

Nutrition Information per Serving:

Carbohydrates: 4.3g

Dietary Fiber: 0.4g

Fat: 19.3g

Protein: 46g

Calories: 501

ITALIAN-INSPIRED CREAMY CHICKEN

Time: 20 minutes

Servings: 4

Ingredients:

⅓ cup of unsweetened coconut cream or unsweetened almond cream

1 teaspoon of olive oil

1 tablespoon of organic minced onion

1 cup of homemade low-sodium chicken broth

1 tablespoon of organic basil pesto

1 tablespoon of organic Italian seasoning

1½ tablespoons of arrowroot powder

2 tablespoons of organic minced garlic

4 boneless and skinless chicken thighs

Pepper

Pinch of salt

Fresh parsley

Instructions:

1. Set the Instant Pot on sauté mode, then pour in the olive oil.
2. When it gets hot, add the garlic and onions then cook for 2 minutes. Add the chicken and cook each side for 2 minutes until the chicken turns golden brown. Use the pepper, salt, and Italian seasoning to season. Add the broth and stir.
3. Lock and seal the lid. Set on Manual and cook for 8 minutes on high pressure.
4. Afterwards, release the pressure naturally for 5 minutes, then quick release the remaining pressure. Take off the lid.
5. Set on Sauté mode then add the arrowroot powder and stir properly to coat the ingredients. Whisk in the basil pesto and coconut cream, then stir. Let it simmer under it gets thicker. Add seasoning to taste.
6. Serve in 4 bowls and use fresh parsley to garnish each serving.

Nutrition Information per Serving:

Carbohydrates: 5.3g

Dietary Fiber: 1.8g

Fat: 15g

Protein: 26g

Calories: 242

FISH AND SEAFOOD RECIPES

LEMON-DILL SALMON FILLET

Time: 20 minutes

Servings: 4

Ingredients:

1 cup of water

1 pound of organic wild-caught salmon fillet

2 cloves of garlic (minced)

2 medium lemon (thinly sliced)

3 tablespoons of ghee

5 large fresh sprigs of dill

12 asparagus (trimmed and sliced into 1-inch pieces)

Pepper

Pinch of salt

Instructions:

- Drizzle the two sides of the salmon with ghee then use pepper and salt to season.
- Put the water, minced garlic, and fresh dill into the Instant Pot. Place a trivet in the pot.
- Place the salmon on the trivet then place layers of lemon slices on it.
- Close and seal the lid. Set on Manual and cook for 4 minutes on high pressure.
- Quick release the pressure when done, then take off the lid.
- Move the salmon to a serving platter. Take out the trivet and pour away the liquid.

- Set the Instant Pot on Sauté mode then put 2 tablespoons of ghee left in the pot.
- Put the asparagus in the pot and cook for 4 minutes. Use pepper and salt to season to taste.
- Cut the salmon into 4 equal pieces the garnish each piece with the asparagus.

Nutrition Information per Serving:

Carbohydrates: 5.4g

Dietary Fiber: 2.7g

Fat: 16.7g

Protein: 24.6g

Calories: 260

CAJUN TILAPIA

Time: 13 minutes

Servings: 4

Ingredients:

1 cup of water

1 teaspoon of dried thyme

1 teaspoon of dried oregano

1 cup of ghee or non-dairy butter (melted)

2 teaspoons of cayenne pepper

2 tablespoons of smoked paprika

2 teaspoons of garlic powder

2 teaspoons of onion powder

4 x 6-ounce of tilapia fillets

Pepper

Pinch of salt

Instructions:

- Get a small bowl and put the cayenne pepper, garlic powder, smoked paprika, dried oregano, dried thyme, onion powder, pepper, and salt in it. Put the melted ghee inside and mix properly.
- Dip each fillet of the tilapia in the seasoned ghee.
- Pour in a cup of water, then place a steamer tack in the Instant Pot. Place the seasoned fillets on the rack.
- Close and seal the lid. Set on Manual and cook for 5 minutes on high pressure.
- Afterwards, when it is done, release the pressure naturally. Take off the lid.
- Move to a platter. Use the fresh parsley and lemon wedges to garnish it. Then serve.

Nutrition Information per Serving:

Carbohydrates: 9.31g

Dietary Fiber: 0.98g

Fat: 26g

Protein: 28.93g

Calories: 383

LEMON SALMON

Time: 16 minutes

Servings: 4

Ingredients:

½ medium fresh lemon (thinly sliced)

1 cup of water

1 tablespoon of ghee (melted)

1 pound of skin-on salmon fillets

Fresh basil

Pinch of salt

White pepper

Fresh parsley

Fresh tarragon

Sprigs of fresh dill

Instructions:

- Add a cup of water and some herbs into the Instant Pot then place the steamer rack in it.
- Use salt and white pepper to season the salmon then drizzle over with the melted ghee.
- Place the fillets on the steamer rack. Then keep the lemon slices on top.
- Close and seal the lid. Set the Instant Pot on "Steam", then cook for 3 minutes on high pressure.
- Release the pressure manually when you are done. Take off the lid.
- Move to a platter then use fresh herbs to garnish it before serving.

Nutrition Information per Serving:

Carbohydrates: 0.7g

Dietary Fiber: 0.2g

Fat: 10.2g

Protein: 22.1g

Calories: 180

GINGER TILAPIA

Time: 23 minutes

Servings: 4

Ingredients:

¼ cup of fresh scallions (julienned)

¼ cup of fresh cilantro (finely chopped)

1 tablespoon of olive oil

1 pound of tilapia fish fillets

2 fresh garlic cloves (finely minced)

2 tablespoons of fresh ginger (julienned)

2 tablespoons of apple cider or white vinegar

3 tablespoons of low-sodium coconut aminos

Pinch of salt

White pepper

Instructions:

- Get a bowl and put the coconut aminos, minced garlic, white peppers, white vinegar, and salt. Stir to mix properly.
- Put the tilapia fish into the bowl. Evenly coat the fish with the sauce then marinate it for 2 hours.
- Pour 2 cups of water into your Instant Pot, then place a steamer rack in it.
- Get the fillets out of the marinade and place them on the steamer rack. Set the marinade aside.
- Close and seal the lid. Set on Manual and cook for 2 minutes on low pressure.
- When it is done, quick release the pressure and take off the lid.
- Move the fillets to a serving dish and get rid of the water.
- Set the Instant Pot on Sauté mode. Heat the olive oil before adding the julienned ginger. Sauté for some seconds. Throw in the cilantro and scallions, then sauté for 2 minutes until it gets soft.
- Add the marinade and stir well to allow it heat properly. Ladle the sauce on the fish then serve.

Nutrition Information per Serving:

Carbohydrates: 4.98g

Dietary Fiber: 0.53g

Fat: 6g

Protein: 25g

Calories: 176

SHRIMP AND SAUSAGE BOIL

Time: 23 minutes

Servings: 6

Ingredients:

½ cup of ghee (melted)

½ teaspoon of garlic powder

1 tablespoon of low-sodium coconut aminos

1 tablespoon of organic Cajun or creole seasoning

1½ pounds of sweet potatoes (peeled, cubed)

1½ pounds shrimp (peeled, deveined)

3 smoked sausage (sliced)

3 cups of homemade low-sodium fish or vegetable broth

Pinch of salt

Pepper

Instructions:

- Put the cubes of sweet potato and sausage in the Instant Pot. Add the low-sodium coconut aminos and broth then stir.
- Lock and seal the lid. Set on Manual and cook for 4 minutes on high pressure.
- Quick release the pressure when you are done. Take off the lid.
- Put the melted ghee, shrimp, black pepper, salt, Cajun seasoning, and garlic powder in the pot. Stir well to mix.
- Let the shrimp heat until it is not pink anymore. Set on Sauté mode as required.
- Scoop into bowls. Garnish each serving with fresh parsley. Serve.

Nutrition Information per Serving:

Carbohydrates: 33.3g

Dietary Fiber: 4.6g

Fat: 38.8g

Protein: 43.1g

Calories: 663

SPICY SHRIMP AND CAULIFLOWER GRITS

Time: 25 minutes

Servings: 4

Ingredients for Cauliflower Grits:

¼ cup of homemade low-sodium chicken broth

1 teaspoon of olive oil

1 cup of unsweetened coconut milk

1 tablespoon of ghee or non-dairy butter

4 cups of grated cauliflower

Pinch of salt

Ingredients for Shrimp:

¼ teaspoon of paprika

¼ cup of onion (finely chopped)

¼ teaspoon of cayenne pepper

1 tablespoon of fresh lemon juice

1 pound of shrimp (peeled and deveined)

2 tablespoons of olive oil

4 bacon slices (finely chopped)

Pepper

Pinch of sea salt

Garnish: 8 cups of fresh swiss chard (sliced), green onions

Instructions:

- Set the Instant Pot on Sauté mode then pour in a teaspoon of olive oil.
- When it gets hot, add the cauliflower. Stir properly while you toast for 3 minutes. Turn off the Sauté mode
- Mix the shrimp ingredients inside a bowl. Stir properly then place the shrimp on the grits.
- Lock and seal the lid. Set on Manual and cook for 10 minutes on high pressure.
- Afterwards, release the pressure naturally for 10 minutes. Take off the lid.
- Place the swiss chard on a serving platter or serving dish. Use shrimp and grits to top it. Use green onions to garnish it. Serve.

Nutrition Information per Serving:

Carbohydrates: 8.46g

Dietary Fiber: 2.1g

Fat: 23.68g

Protein: 30.42g

Calories: 368

CHILI-LIME HALIBUT

Time: 15 minutes

Servings: 2

Ingredients:

1 cup of water

2 x 5-ounces of halibut fillets

Pepper

Pinch of sea salt

Chili-Lime Sauce Ingredients:

½ teaspoon organic cumin

1 tablespoon of melted coconut oil

1 tablespoon of freshly chopped parsley

1 teaspoon of organic smoked paprika

1 medium jalapeno (seeded, peeled, and finely chopped)

Juice from 1 fresh lime

2 cloves of garlic (finely minced)

Small pinch of sea salt

Instruction:

- Put all the ingredients for chili lime sauce together in a bowl. Stir properly before you set it aside.
- Pour a cup of water into the Instant Pot, then place a steamer rack in it.
- Use pepper and salt to season the halibut fillets. Then place the fillets on the steamer rack.
- Lock and seal the lid. Set on Steam mode then cook for 5 minutes on high pressure.
- When it gets done, release the pressure manually. Take off the lid.
- Place the fillets on a serving dish. Drizzle over with chili sauce then serve.

Nutrition Information per Serving:

Carbohydrates: 15.06g

Dietary Fiber: 8.9g

Fat: 25.56g

Protein: 32.75g

Calories: 419

STEAMED CRAB LEGS

Time: 5 minutes

Servings: 4

Ingredients:

½ cup of organic apple cider or white vinegar

1 teaspoon of smoked paprika or regular paprika

2 cups of water

2 pounds of cleaned snow crab legs

2 tablespoons of ghee or coconut oil, melted

4 cloves of garlic (crushed)

Fresh parsley

White pepper

Pinch of sea salt

Juice and zest from 1 medium fresh lemon

Instructions:

- Get a bowl and put the lemon zest, lemon juice, apple cider, ghee, crushed garlic, black pepper, paprika, and salt in it. Stir to mix.
- Pour 2 cups of water into the Instant Pot. Place the steamer rack into the pot.
- Place the snow crab legs on the steamer rack then drizzle over with the lemon mixture.
- Lock and seal the lid. Set on Manual and cook for 2 minutes on high pressure.
- Quick release the pressure when done. Take off the lid.
- Place on a serving platter. Use the fresh parsley to garnish. Serve.

Nutrition Information per Serving:

Carbohydrates: 5g

Dietary Fiber: 0.4g

Fat: 7.9g

Protein: 19.2g

Calories: 176

SWEET CHILI TILAPIA

Time: 10 minutes

Servings: 4

Ingredients:

¼ cup of coconut aminos

2 teaspoons of olive oil

2 teaspoons of crushed red pepper flakes

4 boneless, skinless tilapia fillets

Pepper

Pinch of sea salt

Handful fresh baby spinach (finely chopped)

Topping: ¼ cup of homemade lectin-free chili sauce

1 teaspoon of organic low-sodium coconut aminos

Instructions:

- Get a bowl and mix the coconut aminos, baby spinach, red pepper flakes, black pepper, and salt. Mix properly. Use marinade to completely coat the tilapia fillets.
- Get a second bowl and mix the coconut aminos and chili sauce in it. Stir properly and set aside.
- Set the Instant Pot on Sauté mode, then reduce to the lowest temperature.
- Pour olive oil into the pot. When it gets hot, add the tilapia fillets. Sauté each side for 2 to 3 minutes until thoroughly cooked.

- Place on a serving plate and use the chili sauce as topping. Serve.

Nutrition Information per Serving:

Carbohydrates: 1g

Dietary Fiber: 0g

Fat: 3.4g

Protein: 21.1g

Calories: 118

LOBSTER BISQUE SOUP

Time: 20 minutes

Servings: 6

Ingredients:

1 cup of dry white wine

1 teaspoon of dried thyme

1 cup of celery (finely chopped)

1 cup of carrots (finely chopped)

1 tablespoon of Worcestershire sauce

1 tablespoon of fresh parsley (chopped)

1 medium yellow or red onion (finely chopped)

1 teaspoon of smoked paprika or regular paprika

2 cups of unsweetened coconut cream

2 cups of homemade low-sodium vegetable or fish broth

3 cups of frozen or fresh lobster meat

4 cloves of garlic (minced)

4 tablespoons of organic ghee (clarified butter)

Pepper

Pinch of salt

Instruction:

- Set the Instant Pot on Sauté mode. Melt the ghee in the pot.
- Add celery, onion, garlic, and carrots and cook for 5 minutes.
- Use wine to deglaze the Instant Pot. Let it simmer until it reduces halfway.
- Add the lobster meat and broth. Stir properly.
- Close and seal the lid. Set the pot on Steam mode then cook for 5 minutes on high pressure.
- Release the pressure naturally when done. Take off the lid.
- Add the coconut cream, paprika, Worcestershire sauce, thyme, black pepper, parsley, and salt. Then puree the soup with an immersion blender until it smoothens.
- Spoon the soup into bowls. Use fresh ground black pepper and parsley to garnish. Serve.

Nutrition Information per Serving:

Carbohydrates: 5.3g

Dietary Fiber: 0.67g

Fat: 29.3g

Protein: 24.4g

Calories: 394

PORK RECIPES

TENDER RIBS

Time: 1 hour

Servings: 8

Ingredients:

¼ cup of apple cider vinegar

1 cup of water

1 teaspoon of paprika

1 teaspoon of chili powder

1 teaspoon of garlic powder

1 teaspoon of onion powder

1 tablespoon of Worcestershire sauce

1 tablespoon of low-sodium coconut aminos

2 racks of pork ribs

Pepper

Pinch of salt

Instructions:

- Use the garlic powder, paprika, onion powder, black pepper, chili powder, and salt to season the pork ribs.
- Place the trivet in the Instant Pot. Add the water, coconut aminos, and apple cider vinegar.
- Add the ribs to the trivet. Lock and seal the lid.

- Set on Manual mode then cook for 25 minutes on high pressure.
- Release the pressure naturally when it is done. Take off the lid.
- Move the ribs to a platter. Leave it to rest for 10 minutes. Serve.

Nutrition Information per Serving:

Carbohydrates: 0g

Dietary Fiber: 0g

Fat: 25.08g

Protein: 58.08g

Calories: 475

ADOBO PORK

Time: 1 hour

Servings: 6

Ingredients:

½ pound of green chilies (de-seeded)

½ cup of homemade low-sodium chicken broth or water

½ pound of organic red Fresno peppers or red jalapenos

1 tablespoon of turmeric

1 tablespoon of Adobo seasoning

1 teaspoon of swerve or Erythritol

2 cloves of garlic (crushed)

2 teaspoons of apple cider vinegar

2 pounds of boneless pork shoulder

Pepper

Pinch of salt

Instructions:

- Put the green chilies, garlic cloves, red peppers, apple cider vinegar, swerve, and chicken broth together in a food processor or blender. Blend until it smoothens.
- Put the adobo seasoning, salt, turmeric, and pepper together in a bowl. Mix properly then use it to season all the sides of the pork. Place the pork shoulder in the Instant Pot, then pour over the sauce.
- Lock and seal the lid. Set on Manual then cook for 45 minutes on high pressure.
- Release the pressure naturally when you are done, then take off the lid.
- Place the pork on a serving platter, then use 2 forks to shred it.
- Place it back in the pot and use the sauce to coat it properly. Serve.

Nutrition Information per Serving:

Carbohydrates: 4.8g

Dietary Fiber: 1.1g

Fat: 5.5g

Protein: 40.1g

Calories: 240

HAWAIIAN KALUA PORK

Time: 1 hour and 30 minutes

Servings: 8

Ingredients:

1 teaspoon of freshly cracked black pepper.

1 (20-ounce) can of pineapple chunks in pineapple juice

1 cup of homemade low-sodium beef broth or beef stock

1 medium-sized green cabbage (cored and into six wedges)

1 (5-pound) bone-in or boneless pork shoulder (cut into 3 pieces)

1½ tablespoon of sea salt

3 whole cloves of garlic

6 slices of bacon

Instructions:

- Set the Instant Pot on Sauté and throw in the slices of bacon. Cook all the sides of the bacon before turning off the Sauté mode.
- Make cuts in the pieces of pork and place the whole cloves of garlic in them.
- Sprinkle the pieces with black pepper and salt. Add the pieces of pork to the bacon and pour the pineapple juice and beef broth.
- Lock and seal the lid, then close the valve. Set on Manual and cook on high pressure for 90 minutes.
- Release the pressure naturally after cooking then take off the lid.
- Place the bacon and pork on a serving platter then use two forks to shred them.
- Put the chunks of pineapple and cabbage wedges into the Instant Pot.
- Shut the lid and cook on high pressure for 3 minutes.
- After cooking, quick release the pressure and take off the lid.
- Carefully place the pineapple and cabbage combination on the shredded pork.
- Serve.

Nutrition Information per Serving:

Carbohydrates: 9.5g

Dietary Fiber: 1g

Fat: 16g

Protein: 79.9g

Calories: 518

PORK CHOPS WITH RED CABBAGE

Time: 22 minutes

Servings: 4

Ingredients:

1 tablespoon of olive oil

1 teaspoon of fennel seeds

1 teaspoon of onion powder

1 teaspoon of garlic powder

1 tablespoon of freshly chopped parsley

1 small head of red cabbage (cored and shredded)

2 teaspoons of dried thyme

2 cups of homemade low-sodium chicken broth

3 tablespoons of arrowroot powder

4 pork chops

Pepper

Pinch of salt

Instructions:

- Get a bowl and put the garlic powder, parsley, onion powder, black pepper, fennel seeds, dried thyme, and salt in it. Use these spices to season the pork.
- Set the Instant Pot on Sauté mode and pour in the olive oil.
- Add the pork chops when the oil gets hot. Sear all it sides then take them out of the pot and set aside.
- Put the shredded cabbage and chicken stock into the Instant Pot. Stir properly.
- Add the pork chops to the top of the cabbage.
- Close and seal the lid. Set the Pot on Sauté mode then cook for 8 minutes on high pressure.
- Quick release the pressure after cooking. Take off the lid.
- Place the cabbage and pork chops on a serving platter.
- Set the Instant Pot on Sauté mode. Add the arrowroot powder to the pot and simmer. Stir from time to time until it gets thicker.
- Pour the sauce on the cabbage and pork chops. Serve.

Nutrition Information per Serving:

Carbohydrates: 19.2g

Dietary Fiber: 5.7g

Fat: 23.6g

Protein: 20.9g

Calories: 369

ITALIAN PORK STUFFED SWEET POTATOES

Time: 28 minutes

Servings: 2

Ingredients:

1 teaspoon of garlic powder

1 pound of lean grass-fed ground pork

1 medium yellow onion (finely chopped)

1 tablespoon of fresh parsley (finely chopped)

2 cups of water

2 tablespoons of olive oil

2 medium sweet potatoes

4 cups of fresh kale (roughly chopped)

Pinch of salt

Pepper

Instructions:

- Pour 2 cups of water into the Instant Pot. Place the trivet in the pot and place the sweet potatoes on it.
- Close the lid and seal it. Set on Manual and cook for 15 minutes on high pressure.
- After it is done, release the pressure naturally for 10 minutes. Take off the lid. Take the sweet potatoes out of the Instant Pot. Pour away the water and remove the trivet.
- Set the Instant Pot on Sauté mode, then pour in the olive oil.

- When it gets hot, add the ground pork, parsley, onion, garlic powder, pepper and salt to the pot. Then stir properly.
- Throw in the kale and cook, while stirring occasionally, until it wilts. Turn off the Sauté mode.
- Cut the cooked sweet potatoes into 2 halves then use a spoon to scoop the potato out. Fill the hollow with the ground pork mixture. Serve.

Nutrition Information per Serving:

Carbohydrates: 38.12g

Dietary Fiber: 4.8g

Fat: 21.2g

Protein: 33.12g

Calories: 517

ORANGE SHREDDED PORK

Time: 1 hour 30 minutes

Servings: 8

Ingredients:

⅔ cups of organic apple cider vinegar

½ teaspoon of organic ground cumin

½ cup of fresh parsley (finely chopped)

1 teaspoon of dried oregano

1 medium sweet onion (finely chopped)

1½ cups of fresh orange juice

3 pounds boneless pork butt (cut into 3 equal sized pieces)

4 cloves of garlic (minced)

4 dried ancho chilies (stemmed and seeded)

Pepper

Pinch of sea salt

Instructions:

- Pour the orange juice into the Instant Pot, then add the pieces of pork.
- Close the lid and seal it. Set on Manual and cook for 50 minutes on high pressure.
- After it is done, release the pressure naturally. Take off the lid.
- Place the pieces of pork on a serving platter. Use two forks to shred the pieces, then set them aside.
- Mix the onion, garlic cloves, ancho chilies, apple cider, parsley, vinegar, oregano, black pepper, ground cumin, and salt together in the blender. Blend.
- Set the Instant Pot on Sauté mode, then set on low pressure. Pour in the sauce and allow to simmer, while stirring occasionally, until it gets thicker.
- Throw in the shredded pork and stir until it is evenly coated.
- Place on a platter and serve.

Nutrition Information per Serving:

Carbohydrates: 9.5g

Dietary Fiber: 1.1g

Fat: 6.1g

Protein: 45.9g

Calories: 295

SPICY SPINACH AND PORK STEW

Time: 40 minutes

Servings: 4

Ingredients:

½ cup of organic heavy cream

1 teaspoon of dried thyme

1 large red onion (peeled and finely chopped)

1 pound of boneless pork stewing meat (cut into bite-sized pieces)

1½ cups of homemade low-sodium vegetable broth

4 cloves of garlic (minced)

6 cups of fresh baby spinach, coarsely chopped

Pepper

Pinch of sea salt

Instructions:

- Put the onion, vegetable broth, and garlic in a blender or food processor and blend until very smooth.
- Pour the blended mixture into the Instant Pot and throw in the pork pieces.
- Close the lid and seal it. Set on Manual and cook for 20 minutes on high pressure.
- After you are done, release the pressure naturally then take off the lid.
- Set on Sauté mode. Add the salt, pepper, baby spinach dried thyme, and heavy cream to the pot. Stir while cooking, until the spinach wilts.
- Place on a platter and serve.

Nutrition Information per Serving:

Carbohydrates: 9.23g

Dietary Fiber: 1.98g

Fat: 16.35g

Protein: 24g

Calories: 295

SWEDISH-INSPIRED PORK ROAST

Time: 1 hour 30 minutes

Servings: 8

Ingredients:

½ teaspoon of organic ground cardamom powder

1 tablespoon of olive oil

1 teaspoon of fresh ground nutmeg

1 large yellow onion (peeled and grated)

1 teaspoon of freshly cracked black pepper

1 teaspoon of organic ground cumin powder

1 tablespoon of finely chopped fresh parsley

2 tablespoons of sea salt

2 cups of homemade low-sodium beef broth

3 tablespoons of swerve or Erythritol sweetener

4 pounds of boneless pork loin roast

8 cloves of garlic (crushed)

Instructions:

- Use swerve, cumin powder, pepper, cardamom powder, and salt to season the pork loin roast.
- Set the Instant Pot on Sauté mode then pour in the olive oil.
- When it gets hot, add the garlic and onions then cook for 4 minutes.
- Throw in the pork roast and sear all the sides. Add the beef broth and stir.
- Lock the lid and seal it. Set on Manual and cook for 85 minutes on high pressure.
- When it gets done, release the pressure naturally then take off the lid.
- Place the roast on a serving platter. Allow resting for 10 minutes. Slice and spoon the liquid on the slices. Serve.

Nutrition Information per Serving:

Carbohydrates: 5.5g

Dietary Fiber: 0.3g

Fat: 6.7g

Protein: 48.7g

Calories: 287

PULLED PORK SOUP

Time: 45 minutes

Servings: 6

Ingredients:

½ cup of unsweetened coconut cream

1 large red onion (diced)

1½ pounds of organic cauliflower florets

1½ pound organic boneless whole pork shoulder

2 tablespoons of olive oil

7 cups of homemade low-sodium chicken or pork broth

8 cloves of garlic (minced)

Pepper

Pinch of salt

Instructions:

- Set the Instant Pot on Sauté mode then put 1 tablespoon of olive oil in it.
- When it gets hot, add the pork shoulder and sear all its side.
- Add the tablespoon of olive oil left. Add the onion and cloves of garlic when the oil gets hot then cook for 5 minutes. Add the cauliflower, broth, pepper and salt, then stir.
- Close the lid. Set the pot on Manual and cook for 45 minutes on high pressure.
- After cooking, release the pressure naturally for 10 minutes, then quick release any pressure left. Take off the lid.
- Place the pork shoulder on a cutting board and use two forks to shred it.
- Use an immersion blender to pulse the cauliflower mixture in the Instant Pot. When it is smooth, stir in the coconut cream and pulled pork. Season to taste.
- Scoop into bowls and serve.

Nutrition Information per Serving:

Carbohydrates: 14.8g

Dietary Fiber: 5g

Fat: 24.6g

Protein: 34g

Calories: 409

PORK AND CABBAGE BOWL

Time: 15 minutes

Servings: 6

Ingredients:

1 cup of homemade low-sodium chicken broth

1½ pounds of ground pork

2 tablespoons of olive oil

2 cloves of garlic (minced)

2 shallots (peeled and finely chopped)

2 cups of cauliflower florets (finely chopped)

6 cups of fresh green cabbage (finely shredded)

Pepper

Pinch of salt

Instructions:

- Set the Instant Pot on Sauté mode then pour in the olive oil.
- When it gets hot, add the finely chopped shallots, minced garlic, and ground pork. Cook, while occasionally stirring, until the pork becomes brown. Then turn off Sauté mode.
- Put the cabbage, cauliflower, black pepper, and salt in the Instant Pot.
- Shut the lid and seal it. Set on Manual and cook for 3 minutes on high pressure.
- Afterward, quick release the pressure and take the lid off.
- Place on a platter and serve.

Nutrition Information per Serving:

Carbohydrates: 8.6g

Dietary Fiber: 3.85g

Fat: 4g

Protein: 21g

Calories: 163

BEEF RECIPES
SLOPPY JOES

Time: 16 minutes

Servings: 4

Ingredients:

¼ cup of red wine vinegar

¼ cup of Worcestershire sauce

¼ cup of low-sodium coconut aminos

1 teaspoon of paprika

1 teaspoon of chili powder

1 large onion (finely chopped)

2 tablespoons of olive oil

2½ pounds of organic grass-fed lean ground beef

Pepper

Pinch of salt

Sauce ingredients:

⅓ cup of dried basil

⅓ cup of dried parsley

1 cup of carrots (diced)

1 x 8-ounce can of beets

1 cup of water or chicken broth

1 cup of organic pumpkin puree

1 tablespoon of balsamic vinegar

2 tablespoons of fresh lime juice

4 cloves of garlic (minced)

Instructions:

- Put the sauce ingredients into the blender or food processor and blend until you have a smooth mixture.
- Set the Instant Pot on Sauté mode, then pour in the olive oil.
- Add the onions when the oil gets hot, then cook for 4 minutes.
- Add the ground beef and cook, while occasionally stirring, until the beef is not pink anymore.
- Stir in the coconut aminos, Worcestershire sauce, chili powder, red wine vinegar, paprika, black pepper, and salt.
- Close the lid and seal it. Set the pot on Manual mode then cook for 3 minutes on high pressure.
- After it is done, release the pressure naturally for 15 minutes. Quick release the pressure remaining, then take off the lid.
- Set on Sauté mode and simmer until there is a reduction in the liquid.
- Place on a platter and serve.

Nutrition Information per Serving:

Carbohydrates: 11.23g

Dietary Fiber: 2.8g

Fat: 25.03g

Protein: 45.15g

Calories: 437

WINE AND COFFEE BEEF STEW

Time: 30 minutes

Servings: 8

Ingredients:

⅔ cups of organic red cooking wine

1 medium onion (finely chopped)

1 cup of homemade organic low-sodium beef bone broth

3 tablespoons of coconut oil, avocado oil, olive oil, or ghee

2 cloves of garlic (minced)

2 tablespoons of organic capers

2 tablespoons of arrowroot powder

2 cups of fresh organic mushrooms (sliced)

2½ pounds of organic grass-fed beef chuck stew meat (cut into bite-sized chunks)

3 cups of homemade freshly brewed coffee

Pepper

Pinch of salt

Instructions:

- Set the Instant Pot on Sauté mode, then pour in the oil.

- When the oil gets hot, add the stewing beef in batches (if necessary). Sear all the sides of the beef, take it out of the pot, and set aside.
- Put the onion, garlic, and mushrooms into the pot then cook, while occasionally stirring, until it softens a little. Turn off the Sauté mode.
- Return the beef to the pot, then add the brewed coffee, capers, red cooking wine, beef broth, pepper, and salt.
- Lock the lid and seal it. Set on Manual and cook for 25 minutes on high pressure.
- When cooked, naturally release the pressure and take off the lid.
- Set on Sauté mode then sprinkle arrowroot powder over the ingredients. Let the stew simmer until the liquid becomes thicker and reduces.
- Add the beef to the Instant Pot and stir properly to coat with the mixture.
- Move to a platter and serve.

Nutrition Information per Serving:

Carbohydrates: 1.35g

Dietary Fiber: 0.3g

Fat: 13.28g

Protein: 30.13g

Calories: 242

GARLIC AND ROSEMARY RIB EYE ROAST

Time: 1 hour

Servings: 6

Ingredients:

¼ cup of fresh rosemary

¼ cup of fresh parsley (finely chopped)

1 x 3-pound of boneless organic rib eye beef roast (cut into large pieces)

2 cups of homemade beef broth or water

4 tablespoons of olive oil

4 medium onions (sliced)

4 cups of mushrooms (sliced)

4 tablespoons of ghee (melted)

10 cloves of garlic (minced)

Pepper

Pinch of salt

Instructions:

- Use pepper and salt to season the beef chunks.
- Put the parsley, garlic, melted ghee, and rosemary into a bowl. Mix properly.
- Set the Instant Pot on Sauté mode and put 2 tablespoons of olive oil in it.
- Put the pieces of beef in the pot and sear all the sides. Place the pieces of beef on a cutting board then use the herb mixture and garlic to brush all the pieces.
- Put the 2 tablespoons of olive oil remaining in the Pot and add sliced onions. Cook, while occasionally stirring, until it turns brown. Turn off the Sauté mode.
- Put the mushrooms, beef broth, and pieces of beef roast into the Instant Pot.
- Lock the lid and seal it. Set the pot on Manual then cook for 40 minutes on high pressure.
- After cooking, naturally release the pressure and take off the lid.
- Take the beef out of the Instant Pot and place it on a platter.
- Puree the sauce with an immersion blender. Pour the sauce on the beef chunks and serve.

Nutrition Information per Serving:

Carbohydrates: 11g

Dietary Fiber: 2g

Fat: 22g

Protein: 52g

Calories: 445

EASY TACO MEAT

Time: 15 minutes

Servings: 6

Ingredients:

⅓ cup of fresh cilantro (finely chopped)

1 teaspoon of cumin

1 tablespoon of dried basil

1 tablespoon of chili powder

1 tablespoon of dried oregano

1 teaspoon of regular paprika or smoked paprika

2 medium organic red onions (finely chopped)

2 pounds lean, organic, grass-fed ground beef

4 tablespoons of coconut oil or olive oil

6 cloves of garlic (minced)

Pepper

Pinch of salt

Instructions:

- Set the Instant Pot on Sauté mode and pour in the oil.
- When it gets hot, put the onion in it and cook for 3 minutes. Add the garlic and cook for 2 minutes. Add the ground beef and cook while occasionally stirring, until it browns.
- Put the remaining ingredients, apart from the cilantro, in the Instant Pot. Stir.
- Lock the lid and seal it. Set on Manual and cook for 9 minutes on high pressure.
- When it is cooked, release the pressure naturally. Take off the lid.
- Set the pot on Sauté mode then let it simmer until the liquid reduces.
- Put in a bowl and use fresh cilantro to garnish. Then serve.

Nutrition Information per Serving:

Carbohydrates: 6.3g

Dietary Fiber: 1.84g

Fat: 34.2g

Protein: 29.1g

Calories: 442

BEEF MEATBALLS WITH MUSHROOM SAUCE

Time: 24 minutes

Servings: 6

Ingredients:

¼ cup of fresh parsley (chopped)

½ cup of unsweetened coconut cream

2 pounds of lean grass-fed ground beef

1 medium carrot (grated)

1 tablespoon of dried oregano

1 yellow onion (finely chopped)

1 tablespoon of smoked or regular paprika

2 large eggs

2 cups of mushrooms

2 tablespoons of olive oil

2 tablespoons of mustard

2 tablespoons of arrowroot powder

2 cups of homemade low-sodium beef broth

Pinch of salt

Pepper

Instructions:

- Put the ground beef, grated carrots, onion, egg, dried oregano, arrowroot powder mustard, paprika, black pepper, and salt in a large bowl. Stir well.
- Mold the ground beef mixture into meatballs. Set them aside.
- Set the Instant Pot on Sauté mode, then pour in the olive oil.
- When it gets hot, put the meatballs in a single layer into the pot. Cook until all the sides are brown.
- Add the beef broth and mushrooms.
- Close the lid and seal it. Set on Manual and cook for 16 minutes on high pressure.
- When it is cooked, release the pressure naturally for 10 minutes. Take off the lid.
- Place the meatballs on a serving platter.
- Pulse the mushrooms with an immersion blender until it is smooth. Add the coconut cream and parsley then stir.
- Scoop the mushroom sauce on the meatballs and serve.

Nutrition Information per Serving:

Carbohydrates: 8.06g

Dietary Fiber: 1.4g

Fat: 32.07g

Protein: 46.88g

Calories: 514

MEATLOAF WITH PUMPKIN BARBECUE SAUCE

Time: 33 minutes

Servings: 8

Meatloaf Ingredients:

½ red onion (finely chopped)

1 teaspoon of chili powder

1 tablespoon of smoked paprika

1 cup of organic pureed pumpkins

1 teaspoon of organic cinnamon powder

2 eggs

2½ pounds of organic grass-fed lean ground beef

3 cloves of garlic (minced)

Pepper

Pinch of salt

Pumpkin Barbecue Glaze Ingredients:

½ teaspoon of salt

½ cup of molasses

1 cup of organic pureed pumpkins

2 tablespoons of Worcestershire sauce

2 tablespoons of organic lectin-free mustard

2 tablespoons of apple cider vinegar

1 tablespoon of parsley, thyme, or oregano

2 teaspoons of organic ground cinnamon powder

Instructions:

- Mix all the ingredients for the pumpkin barbecue glaze together in a bowl. Set it aside.
- Mix the ingredients for the meatloaf together in another big bowl. Stir properly.
- Use the mixture of beef to form a loaf, then place it on an aluminum foil sheet. Pour the pumpkin sauce on the meatloaf, then use the aluminum foil to wrap the meatloaf.
- Pour a cup of water into the Instant Pot and place a trivet on it. Place the meatloaf on the trivet.
- Lock the lid and seal it. Set on Manual and cook for 20 minutes on high pressure.
- When it is cooked, quick release the pressure and take off the lid.
- Take off the foil from the meatloaf. Let it rest for 5 minutes. Slice and serve.

Nutrition Information per Serving:

Carbohydrates: 20.33g

Dietary Fiber: 1.9g

Fat: 26.61g

Protein: 45.95g

Calories: 489

BEEF CURRY

Time: 46 minutes

Servings: 6

Ingredients:

½ cup of homemade low-sodium bone broth

1 onion (finely chopped)

1 teaspoon of paprika

1 teaspoon of dried oregano

1 cup of unsweetened coconut cream

1 pound of organic grass-fed boneless beef stewing meat, cut into bite-sized pieces

2 tablespoons of curry powder

2 tablespoons of arrowroot powder

2 tablespoons of olive oil, coconut oil, or ghee

3 large sweet potatoes (cubed)

4 cloves of garlic (minced)

6 carrots (peeled and cut into bite-sized pieces)

Pepper

Pinch of salt

Instructions:

- Set the Instant Pot on Sauté mode, then pour in the cooking oil.
- When it gets hot, add the garlic and onions. Sauté and occasionally stir until it is browned a little.
- Put the beef stewing in the pot. Cook while occasionally stirring, until all the sides are brown. Turn off Sauté mode.
- Add the carrots, salt, curry powder, black pepper, paprika, dried oregano, bone broth, and coconut cream. Stir properly.
- Lock the lid and seal it. Set on Manual then cook for 30 minutes on high pressure.
- When it is done, either naturally release or quick release the pressure. Take off the lid.
- Place the meat on a platter then add the arrowroot powder. Stir well then leave it to thicken.

- Put the meat back into the sauce and stir until the meat is well coated.
- Place on a platter then use fresh celery to garnish before serving.

Nutrition Information per Serving:

Carbohydrates: 13.3g

Dietary Fiber: 4g

Fat: 25.7g

Protein: 29g

Calories: 398

BEEF BURGUNDY WITH MUSHROOMS

Time: 43 minutes

Servings: 6

Ingredients

½ cup of homemade low-sodium beef broth

1 cup of red wine

1 teaspoon of fresh thyme

1 yellow onion (finely chopped)

1½ cups of mushrooms (sliced)

2 bay leaves

2 pounds of organic beef chuck roast (cut into bite-sized pieces)

3 tablespoons of almond flour

3 tablespoons of coconut oil, olive oil, or avocado oil

4 cloves of garlic (minced)

4 carrots (peeled and cut into bite-sized pieces)

Pepper

Pinch of salt

Instructions:

- Use pepper and salt to season the pieces of beef. Use almond flour to coat lightly.
- Set on Sauté mode and pour in the olive oil.
- When it gets hot, add the onions then cook for 3 minutes. Add the garlic and cook for 2 minutes. Add the pieces of beef and sear all the sides. Take them out of the pot and set aside.
- Use red wine to deglaze the Instant Pot. Scrape off brown bits in the pot then simmer so the red wine reduces by half.
- Put the beef back into the Instant Pot. Add the broth, carrots, thyme, bay leaves, and mushroom.
- Lock the lid and seal it. Set on Manual and cook for 40 minutes on high pressure.
- After cooking, release the pressure naturally for 10 minutes, then quick release any pressure left. Take off the lid and take the bay leaves out of the pot.
- Season then place on a platter and serve.

Nutrition Information per Serving:

Carbohydrates: 5.07g

Dietary Fiber: 1.5g

Fat: 15.89g

Protein: 35g

Calories: 288

FAJITA STEAK BOWL

Time: 17 minutes

Servings: 6

Ingredients:

1 teaspoon of chili powder

1 tablespoon of fresh lime juice

1 cup of organic low-sodium beef broth

2 tablespoons of olive oil

2½ pounds of organic fajita steak (cut into bite-sized pieces)

4 cloves of garlic (minced)

4 avocados (peeled, nut removed, diced)

Pepper

Pinch of salt

Instructions:

- Set the Instant Pot on Sauté mode and pour in the olive oil.
- When it gets hot, put the garlic in the pot and let it sauté for 2 minutes.
- Throw in the pieces of steak and cook until it is almost brown.
- Put the other ingredients left into the pot and stir properly.
- Lock the lid and seal it. Set on Manual and cook for 10 minutes on high pressure.
- When it is cooked, quick release the pressure and take the lid off.

- Turn off the Sauté mode and allow to simmer until almost all the liquid evaporates.
- Place the pieces of steak and diced avocado into a bowl. Serve.

Nutrition Information per Serving:

Carbohydrates: 13.5g

Dietary Fiber: 9.1g

Fat: 40.3g

Protein: 48.8g

Calories: 603

CHUCK ROAST STEW

Time: 35 minutes

Servings: 8

Ingredients:

½ pounds of organic bacon strips (finely chopped)

1 sweet potato (cubed)

1 tablespoon of Worcestershire sauce

1 cup of homemade low-sodium beef broth

1 small purple cabbage (cored and shredded)

2 carrots (thinly sliced)

2 celery ribs (chopped)

2 tablespoons of olive oil

2 large red onions (sliced)

2 tablespoons of arrowroot powder

3 cloves of garlic (crushed)

3 pounds of lean grass-fed chuck roast (cut into bite-sized pieces)

Pepper

Pinch of salt

Ingredients:

- Set the Instant Pot on Sauté mode. When it gets hot, cook the bacon in it until it browns. Set the bacon aside.
- While the pot is still on Sauté mode, add the chuck roast pieces and sear all the sides. Take the pieces out of the pot and set them aside.
- Put the onion, celery, garlic, carrots, and sweet potatoes in the Instant Pot and cook for 5 minutes.
- Put the beef and bacon back into the pot. Throw in the broth, Worcestershire sauce, cabbage, salt and pepper.
- Lock the lid and seal it. Set on Manual mode and cook for 28 minutes on high pressure.
- When it is cooked, release the pressure naturally and take off the lid. Place the roast pieces in a bowl.
- Set on Sauté mode then sprinkle the arrowroot powder in the pot then allow to simmer until the liquid gets thicker.
- Place the pieces back into the pot and stir until they are evenly coated. Place on a platter and serve.

Nutrition Information per Serving:

Carbohydrates: 5.83g

Dietary Fiber: 2g

Fat: 23.2g

Protein: 38g

Calories: 375

LAMB RECIPES

HONG-KONG LAMB

Time: 30 minutes

Servings: 6

Ingredients:

¼ cup of Zhu Hou sauce

1 cup of celery (diced)

1 cup of shredded bok choy

1 organic bamboo shoot (peeled, thinly sliced)

2 tablespoons of oyster sauce

2½ pounds of boneless lamb breasts, cut into bite-sized pieces

3 tablespoons of Shaoxing wine

3 tablespoons of olive oil and coconut oil

3 tablespoons of low-sodium coconut aminos

4 small carrots (diced)

4 cups of homemade low-sodium chicken broth or water

6 scallions (chopped)

6 large dried Shiitake mushrooms

13 thin slices of fresh peeled ginger

Pepper

Pinch of salt

Instructions:

- Soak the shiitake mushrooms in water for 30 minutes. Afterward, remove it and keep the water. Cut the mushrooms into 2 halves.
- Set the Instant Pot on Sauté mode and put 2 tablespoons of oil in the pot.
- When it gets hot, put the lamb pieces, in batches, into the pot and sear all the sides. Set it aside.
- Pour the remaining oil into the pot, then add the ginger and scallions. Sauté for 3 minutes.
- Place the lamb back into the pot with the other ingredients left.
- Close the lid and seal it. Set on Manual and cook for 15 minutes on high pressure.
- When it is cooked, naturally release the pressure then take the lid off. Stir well and season to taste. Scoop into bowls then use fresh parsley to garnish. Serve.

Nutrition Information per Serving:

Carbohydrates: 8.2g

Dietary Fiber: 2g

Fat: 21.2g

Protein: 54.7g

Calories: 457

SWEET POTATO AND LAMB STEW

Time: 50 minutes

Servings: 6

Ingredients:

1 cinnamon stick

1 teaspoon of organic cumin powder

1 medium yellow onion (finely chopped)

1 tablespoon of organic pureed pumpkin

1 tablespoon of fresh parsley (finely chopped)

1 cup of homemade low-sodium chicken broth

1 pound of sweet potatoes (peeled and cubed)

2 tablespoon of olive oil

2 teaspoons of organic ground coriander powder

2 pounds of boneless lamb shoulder (cut into bite-sized pieces)

2-inches of fresh organic ginger root (peeled and finely chopped)

4 cloves of garlic (thinly sliced)

Pinch of salt

Pepper

Instructions:

- Mix the cumin, pepper, coriander, and salt together in a bowl. Use lamb with spice mix to season it.
- Set the Instant Pot on Sauté mode and pour in the olive oil.
- When it gets hot, put the lamb pieces into the pot in batches. Cook each batch until they are browned. Take them out of the pot and set aside.
- Put the onions in the Instant Pot and cook for 4 minutes. Add garlic and cook for 2 minutes. Stir in the ginger and pureed pumpkin and sauté for 1 minute. Consistently stir.
- Put the chicken broth and cinnamon stick into the Instant Pot.

- Close the lid and seal it. Set on Manual and cook for 25 minutes on high pressure.
- After cooking, release the pressure naturally and take the lid off.
- Put the sweet potatoes in the pot. Close the lid and seal it and then cook for 10 minutes on high pressure.
- After cooking, quick release the pressure. Take off the lid and take out the cinnamon stick.
- Move to bowls then use fresh parsley to garnish. Serve.

Nutrition Information per Serving:

Carbohydrates: 21g

Dietary Fiber: 4g

Fat: 16g

Protein: 43g

Calories: 410

LEG OF LAMB WITH MUSHROOM GRAVY

Time: 2 hours

Servings: 8

Ingredients:

½ cup of white wine

1 tablespoon of dried thyme

1 tablespoon of fresh parsley

1 tablespoon of garlic powder

1 tablespoon of onion powder

1 tablespoon of dried oregano

2 cups of mushrooms

2 tablespoons of arrowroot powder

2 tablespoons of coconut oil or olive oil

3 tablespoons of non-dairy butter or ghee

4 cups of water

4 pounds of boneless leg of lamb

Pinch of salt

Pepper

Instructions:

- Mix the thyme, garlic powder, oregano, onion powder, black pepper, parsley, and salt together in a bowl. Then use the spice mix to season the leg of lamb.
- Set the Instant Pot on Sauté mode and pour in the olive oil.
- When the oil gets hot, sear all the sides of the leg of lamb. Remove them from the pot and set aside.
- Use the white wine to deglaze the Instant Pot. Simmer until it reduces halfway then scrape off the browned bits stuck to the pot. Turn off the pot's Sauté mode.
- Put the mushrooms and water into the Instant Pot. Place the leg of lamb back into the pot.
- Lock the lid and seal it. Make sure you close the valve. Set the pot on Manual then cook on high pressure for 90 minutes.
- When cooked, naturally release the pressure and take off the lid. Get the lamb out and set it aside.
- Use an immersion blender to blend the mushroom and liquid. When smooth, stir in the arrowroot powder and let it thicken. Place the lamb back into the pot and stir to coat it with the mixture.
- Place on a platter and serve.

Nutrition Information per Serving:

Carbohydrates: 1g

Dietary Fiber: 0.2g

Fat: 25g

Protein: 64g

Calories: 510

LAMB MEATBALLS

Time: 16 minutes

Servings: 6

Ingredients:

¼ cup of fresh parsley (finely chopped)

¼ cup of fresh rosemary (finely chopped)

½ cup of dry white wine

1 teaspoon of black pepper

1 tablespoon of Cajun seasoning

1 cup of homemade low-sodium chicken broth

1 teaspoon of organic ground cinnamon powder

2 large eggs

2 teaspoons of sea salt

2 tablespoons of olive oil

2 pounds of extra lean grass-fed ground lamb

2 tablespoons of almond flour or coconut flour

2 tablespoons of unsweetened coconut cream or organic heavy cream

4 minced garlic cloves

6 medium shallots (peeled and finely chopped)

Instructions:

- Mix the ground lamb, garlic, egg, shallots, coconut flour, cinnamon powder, cream, parsley, rosemary, Cajun seasoning, pepper, and salt together in a large bowl.
- Use the mixture to form meatballs then set them aside.
- Set the Instant Pot on Sauté mode then pour in the olive oil.
- When the oil gets hot, place the lamb meatballs in the pot in batches. Cook each batch until they are brown. Turn off sauté mode.
- Place the meatballs back into the Instant Pot. Add the wine and chicken broth. Close the lid and seal it. Set on Manual and cook for 8 minutes on high pressure.
- After it is cooked, quick release the pressure and take off the lid.
- Stir properly before placing the meatballs on a platter. Serve.

Nutrition Information per Serving:

Carbohydrates: 14g

Dietary Fiber: 2g

Fat: 19g

Protein: 47g

Calories: 437

SYRIAN-STYLE SHAKRIYEH – LAMB YOGURT STEW

Time: 1 hour

Servings: 6

Ingredients:

1 large red onion or yellow onion (finely chopped)

2 tablespoons of arrowroot powder

2 cups of unsweetened coconut yogurt or goat yogurt

2 pounds of boneless lamb shoulder (cut into bite-sized pieces)

4 tablespoons of sea salt (divided)

4 tablespoons of toasted pine nuts (for garnishing)

8 cups of homemade low-sodium chicken broth or water

Instructions:

- Put the chicken broth, lamb pieces, and 2 tablespoons of salt into the Instant Pot.
- Lock the lid and seal it. Set on Manual and cook for 40 minutes on high pressure.
- After cooking, either quick release or naturally release the pressure. Take off the lid.
- Take the lamb pieces out of the pot.
- Put the yogurt, arrowroot powder, and salt into a blender. Blend until smooth.
- Set the Instant Pot on Sauté mode. Stir in the yogurt mixture and liquid slowly. Let it simmer until it mixes and gets thicker. Put the cooked lamb back into the pot and simmer for 3 minutes.
- Place the lamb and sauce on a serving platter. Use toasted pine nuts to garnish. Serve.

Nutrition Information per Serving:

Carbohydrates: 17g

Dietary Fiber: 1g

Fat: 17g

Protein: 53g

Calories: 459

LAMB ROGAN

Time: 15 minutes

Servings: 4

Ingredients:

¼ cup of unsweetened coconut milk yogurt

½ teaspoon of organic chili powder

1 teaspoon of salt

1 cup of pureed pumpkin

1 teaspoon of cumin seeds

1 teaspoon of fennel seeds

1 tablespoon of coconut oil

1 teaspoon of organic ground cumin

1 teaspoon of organic ground ginger

1 teaspoon of ground cinnamon powder

1 tablespoon of fresh coriander (finely chopped)

1 pound of lamb stewing meat (cut into 2-inch pieces)

1½ teaspoons of organic garam masala

2 bay leaves

2 garlic cloves (minced)

3 green cardamom pods (opened)

Instructions:

- Put the lamb stewing meat, garam masala, and coconut milk yogurt together in a bowl. Stir well to coat then keep in the refrigerator. Marinate overnight.
- Set the Instant Pot on Sauté mode then pour in the coconut oil.
- When it gets hot, add the garlic and cook for 2 minutes. Then add the lamb pieces and sear on all sides.
- Lock the lid and seal it. Set on Manual and cook for 9 minutes on high pressure.
- When it is cooked, quick release the pressure and then take off the lid. Take the bay leaves out.
- Turn off the Sauté mode and allow to simmer until the liquid gets to its desired consistency. Season to taste then pour into bowls. Use fresh coriander to garnish before serving.

Nutrition Information per Serving:

Carbohydrates: 8g

Dietary Fiber: 3g

Fat: 6.9g

Protein: 18g

Calories: 199

LAMB SHAWARMA

Time: 27 minutes

Servings: 8

Ingredients:

½ cup of coconut oil

1 teaspoon of fennel seeds

1 tablespoon of cumin seeds

1 tablespoon of nutmeg (finely grated)

1 cup of fresh cilantro (finely chopped)

1 tablespoon of dried sumac seasoning

1 3-inch fresh ginger (peeled and finely minced)

1 tablespoon of regular paprika or smoked paprika

2 teaspoons of organic ground cinnamon powder

4 garlic cloves (minced)

4 tablespoons of fresh lime juice

5 pounds of boneless lamb shoulder

Pepper

Pinch of salt

Instructions:

- Mix the coconut oil, paprika, lime juice, ground cinnamon, cumin seeds, fennel seeds, fresh cilantro, sumac, nutmeg, pepper, garlic, salt, and ginger together in either a large mixing bowl or a large Ziploc bag.
- Put the lamb shoulder in the covered bowl or Ziploc then place in the fridge overnight to marinate.
- When you are ready to cook, place the marinade and lamb in the Instant Pot.
- Lock the lid and seal it. Set on Manual and cook for 9 minutes on high pressure.
- After cooking, release the pressure naturally for 15 minutes, then quick release any pressure left. Take off the lid.
- Place the lamb on a platter. Carve after 10 minutes. Serve.

Nutrition Information per Serving:

Carbohydrates: 3.2g

Dietary Fiber: 1g

Fat: 72.23g

Protein: 63.1g

Calories: 983

LAMB STEW

Time: 29 minutes

Servings: 4

Ingredients:

¼ cup of tahini sauce

½ cup of fresh mint (finely chopped)

½ cup of fresh parsley (finely chopped)

1 teaspoon of pepper

1 medium yellow onion (finely chopped)

1 cup of homemade low-sodium chicken broth

1 pound of lamb stewing meat (cut into bite-sized pieces)

1 pound of fresh asparagus (trimmed and cut into 1-inch pieces)

2 teaspoons of salt

2 tablespoons of ghee or non-dairy butter

6 garlic cloves (minced)

Juice and zest from 1 medium lemon

Instructions:

- In your Instant Pot, add the non-diary butter or ghee, lamb stew meat, minced garlic, finely chopped yellow onion, chicken broth, black pepper, and salt.
- Lock the lid and seal it. Set on Manual and cook for 16 minutes on high pressure.
- After cooking, release the pressure naturally. Take off the lid.
- Stir in the asparagus pieces, lemon juice and zest, tahini sauce, parsley, and mint. Heat for 5 minutes before transferring to a serving platter. Serve.

Nutrition Information per Serving:

Carbohydrates: 9.1g

Dietary Fiber: 3.9g

Fat: 22.9g

Protein: 37.2g

Calories: 387

CHIPOTLE BRAISED LAMB

Time: 48 minutes

Servings: 4

Ingredients:

1 medium beet

1 teaspoon of pepper

1 tablespoon of sea salt

1 chipotle in adobo sauce

1 tablespoon of garlic powder

1 tablespoon of onion powder

1 medium red onion (thinly sliced)

1 tablespoon of organic ground cumin

1 x 15-ounce can of pureed pumpkin

1 teaspoon of organic ground coriander

1 teaspoon of organic mustard seasoning

1 cup of homemade low-sodium chicken broth

2 garlic cloves (minced)

2 tablespoons of olive oil

4 lamb shanks

4 carrots (peeled and diced)

Instructions:

- Put all the spices and seasonings together in a small bowl. Mix properly.
- Use the seasoning mixture to sprinkle over the lamb shanks.
- Set the Instant Pot on Sauté mode and pour in the olive oil.
- When it gets hot, in batches, sear each side of the lamb shanks for 5 minutes until it is evenly browned. Remove the lamb shanks and set them aside. Turn off Sauté mode.
- Put the chipotle, pureed pumpkin, beet, and chicken broth together in a food processor or blender. Puree until smooth.
- Put the sliced onions, chipotle mixture, and minced garlic in the Instant Pot. Place the lamb shanks on at the top.
- Lock the lid and seal it. Set on Manual and cook for 45 minutes on high pressure.
- After cooking, release the pressure naturally for 15 minutes. Quick release the pressure left then take off the lid.
- Place the lamb on a serving platter.
- Press the Sauté button on the pot. Simmer until it gets thicker, while stirring. Place the lamb back into the pot and stir until the mixture coats it. Serve.

Nutrition Information per Serving:

Carbohydrates: 18.2g

Dietary Fiber: 5.3g

Fat: 31.3g

Protein: 94.1g

Calories: 743

GREEK-STYLE GROUND LAMB GYROS

Time: 50 minutes

Servings: 6

Ingredients:

1 small yellow onion (finely chopped)

1 tablespoon of dried or fresh oregano

1 tablespoon of dried or fresh rosemary

1 tablespoon of organic ground marjoram

2 pounds of lean organic ground lamb

8 whole garlic cloves

Pepper

Pinch salt

Instructions:

- Put the onions, ground marjoram, garlic, rosemary, black pepper, oregano, and salt in a food processor and blend until well mixed.
- Pour the mixture into a large bowl and add the ground lamb. Stir well to mix.
- Get a greased loaf pan that fits into your Instant Pot and press the ground lamb mixture into it. Use aluminum foil to cover securely.
- Pour 2 cups of water into the pot. Place the trivet in the pot then place the loaf pan on the trivet.
- Lock the lid and seal it. Set on Manual and cook for 15 minutes on high pressure.
- After cooking, release the pressure naturally then take off the lid.
- Remove the loaf pan and allow to rest for 5 minutes. Slice and serve.

Nutrition Information per Serving:

Carbohydrates: 1.71g

Dietary Fiber: 0g

Fat: 25.45g

Protein: 37g

Calories: 394

VEGAN AND VEGETABLE RECIPES

SWEET POTATO, CAULIFLOWER, BROCCOLI STIR-FRY

Time: 10 minutes

Servings: 6

Ingredients:

⅛ cup of water

1 medium yellow onion (finely chopped)

1 tablespoon of fresh parsley (finely chopped)

2 medium sweet potatoes (peeled and cubed)

4 garlic cloves (minced)

4 cups of broccoli florets

4 cups of cauliflower florets

4 tablespoons of non-dairy butter or ghee

Pepper

Pinch of salt

Sesame seeds for serving

Instructions:

- Set the Instant Pot on Sauté mode then add the ghee.
- When it gets hot, add the chopped onions and cook for 4 minutes. Add garlic and cook for 2 minutes.

- Add sweet potatoes and cook for 3 minutes. Occasionally stir.
- Add the broccoli, cauliflower, and water.
- Lock the lid and seal it. Set on Manual and cook for 2 minutes on high pressure.
- After cooking, quick release the pressure. Take off the lid and add the parsley, pepper, and salt.
- Place on a platter, garnish with sesame seeds, and serve.

Nutrition Information per Serving:

Carbohydrates: 21g

Dietary Fiber: 5g

Fat: 8g

Protein: 4.83g

Calories: 193

SWEET POTATO CURRY – ALOO SAAG

Time: 30 minutes

Servings: 4

Ingredients:

½ teaspoon of turmeric powder

½ teaspoon of organic cumin seeds

½ teaspoon of garam masala powder

½ teaspoon of ground cumin powder

½-inch of fresh ginger (peeled and grated)

1 cup of fresh baby spinach

1 medium red onion (finely chopped)

1 cup of cauliflower florets (chopped)

2 tablespoons of coconut oil (melted)

2 medium sweet potatoes (peeled and cubed)

2 cups of homemade low-sodium vegetable broth

4 garlic cloves (minced)

Pepper

Pinch of salt

Juice from 1 lime

Instructions:

- Put the spinach, vegetable broth, and ginger together in a food processor or blender. Blend until it reaches the desired consistency, then set aside.
- Set the Instant Pot on Sauté mode then pour in the coconut oil.
- When it gets hot, add the onion and cook for 4 minutes. Add the garlic and cook for 2 minutes.
- Stir in the ingredients left, along with the pureed spinach.
- Lock the lid and seal it. Set on Manual and cook for 4 minutes on high pressure.
- When it is cooked, quick release the pressure and take off the lid.
- Stir well and season to taste. Scoop into bowls and serve.

Nutrition Information per Serving:

Carbohydrates: 14.9g

Dietary Fiber: 4.2g

Fat: 5.3g

Protein: 5.1g

Calories: 110

MUSHROOM STIR-FRY

Time: 33 minutes

Servings: 2

Ingredients:

½ teaspoon of mustard seeds

¼ teaspoon of turmeric powder

1 strand of curry leaves

1 teaspoon of cumin seeds

2 tablespoons of olive oil

3 tablespoons of homemade low-sodium vegetable broth

4 cups of mushrooms (finely sliced)

Pepper

Pinch of salt

Instructions:

- Set the Instant Pot on Sauté mode then pour in the olive oil.

- When it gets hot, add the cumin seeds, curry leaves, salt, mustard seeds, turmeric, pepper, vegetable broth, and mushrooms. Turn off the Sauté mode.
- Close the lid and seal it. Set on Steam mode then cook for 2 minutes on high pressure.
- After cooking, quick release the pressure. Take off the lid.
- Set on Sauté mode and simmer until the liquid evaporates.
- Spoon into bowls. Use fresh parsley to garnish. Serve.

Nutrition Information per Serving:

Carbohydrates: 4.7g

Dietary Fiber: 1.4g

Fat: 14.4g

Protein: 4.4g

Calories: 150

CAULIFLOWER RISOTTO

Time: 10 minutes

Servings: 4

Ingredients:

¼ teaspoon of red pepper flakes

¼ cup of non-dairy butter or ghee

½ bunch chives (thinly sliced)

½ teaspoon of garlic powder

1 teaspoon of fresh thyme

1 cup of fresh baby spinach

1 cup of organic baby carrots

1 teaspoon of fresh lemon zest

1 cup of organic fresh broccoli florets

1 cup of fresh leeks (finely chopped)

1 medium yellow onion (finely chopped)

1½ cups of cauliflower rice

2 garlic cloves (minced)

2 tablespoons of olive oil

2 tablespoons of fresh lemon juice

4 cups of homemade low-sodium vegetable broth

12 asparagus (remove woodsy stem, diced)

Pinch of salt

Pepper

Instructions:

- Use parchment paper to line the baking sheet. Put the asparagus, carrots and broccoli on the tray in a single layer. Drizzle the olive oil over them. Use pepper and salt to season to taste.
- Heat the oven to 400oF and place the baking sheet in it for 15 minutes. When the broccoli is tender, remove it and set aside. Dice into small pieces when it is cooled.
- Set the Instant Pot on Sauté mode then add 1 tablespoon of olive oil to the pot.
- Add the onion once the oil gets hot, then cook for 4 minutes. Add garlic and leeks then cook for 2 minutes. Add the cauliflower rice and sauté for 1 minute.

- Add the vegetable broth, non-dairy butter or ghee, and fresh thyme. Stir to mix.
- Lock the lid and seal it. Set on Manual and cook for 7 minutes on high pressure.
- After cooking, quick release the pressure. Take off the lid.
- Set on Sauté mode again. Stir in the broccoli, asparagus, carrots, spinach, leeks, garlic powder, lemon zest, red pepper flakes, and lemon juice. Sauté for 1 minute, until the spinach becomes wilted. Scoop into bowls then use chives to garnish. Serve.

Nutrition Information per Serving:

Carbohydrates: 15.3g

Dietary Fiber: 4.3g

Fat: 21.5g

Protein: 8.4g

Calories: 278

BARBECUE JACKFRUIT

Time: 16 minutes

Servings: 6

Ingredients:

½ cup of vinegar

1 teaspoon of pepper

1 teaspoon of onion powder

1 teaspoon of garlic powder

1 tablespoon of Worcestershire sauce

1 cup of ghee or non-dairy butter (melted)

1 cup of homemade low-sodium vegetable broth

2 teaspoons of salt

2 teaspoons of paprika

2 x 20-ounce cans jackfruit (drained and chopped)

Juice from 1 fresh lemon

Lettuce leaves for serving

Instructions:

- Put the vegetable broth and jackfruit in the Instant Pot.
- Lock the lid and seal it. Set the pot on Manual then cook for 5 minutes on high pressure.
- After cooking, release the pressure naturally. Take off the lid.
- Use a colander to drain the liquid from the jackfruit. Place the fruit back in the pot. Use a potato masher to slightly smash the fruit.
- Mix the melted ghee, lemon juice, paprika, onion powder, black pepper, vinegar, Worcestershire sauce, garlic powder, and salt together in a bowl. Stir properly. Pour the mixture on the jackfruit.
- Set on Sauté mode then warm them for 5 minutes. Place the lettuce leaves on top. Serve.

Nutrition Information per Serving:

Carbohydrates: 45.7g

Dietary Fiber: 3g

Fat: 34.8g

Protein: 3./g

Calories: 488

MASHED CAULIFLOWER WITH SPINACH

Time: 15 minutes

Servings: 4

Ingredients:

½ cup of organic heavy cream or unsweetened coconut cream

1 tablespoon of flavorless oil

1 cup of homemade vegetable broth

1 small yellow onion (finely chopped)

1 large cauliflower head (cut into florets)

2 cloves of garlic (minced)

2 cups of organic baby spinach

2 tablespoons of nor on-dairy butter ghee

6 sprigs of fresh thyme

Pepper

Pinch of salt

Instructions:

- Set the Instant Pot on Sauté mode then pour in the oil.
- Put the onions and cook for 4 minutes. Then put the garlic and cook for an additional 2 minutes. Add the thyme and stir.

- Pour in a cup of water then place the trivet in the pot. Put the cauliflower on the trivet.
- Lock the lid and seal it. Set on manual then cook for 15 minutes on high pressure.
- Afterward, release the pressure naturally for 10 minutes, then quick release any pressure left. Take off the lid.
- Take out the trivet, pour out the liquid, and place the cauliflower back into the pot.
- As the pot remains hot, add the ghee, black pepper, spinach, and cream together. Use a potato masher to mash all the ingredients until they combine well.
- Season to taste, place on a bowl, and serve.

Nutrition Information per Serving:

Carbohydrates: 9.8g

Dietary Fiber: 4.1g

Fat: 4.3g

Protein: 9.83g

Calories: 111

GARLIC GREEN BEANS

Time: 8 minutes

Servings: 4

Ingredients:

¼ cup of ghee (melted)

½ cup of homemade low-sodium vegetable broth

1 pound of fresh green beans (trimmed, chopped)

6 cloves of garlic (minced)

Pepper

Pinch of salt

Juice from ½ medium fresh lemon

Instructions:

- Set the Instant Pot on Sauté mode then put the ghee in it.
- Add the garlic when the ghee melts. Cook for a minute while occasionally stirring.
- Throw in the green beans. Stir properly before pouring in the vegetable broth.
- Close the lid and seal it. Set on Manual and cook for 5 minutes.
- After cooking, quick release the pressure and take off the lid.
- Squeeze out the fresh lemon juice on top of the green beans. Use pepper and salt to season it.
- Place on a platter and serve.

Nutrition Information per Serving:

Carbohydrates: 45.7g

Dietary Fiber: 3g

Fat: 12.8g

Protein: 3.8g

Calories: 117

MEXICAN-INSPIRED POSOLE

Time: 50 minutes

Servings: 8

Ingredients:

¾ cup of coconut flour or almond flour

½ cup of coconut oil or olive oil

½ cup of New Mexico red chile powder

1 medium yellow onion (finely chopped)

1 large head cauliflower (finely chopped)

1 teaspoon of organic ground cumin powder

1 teaspoon of organic Mexican dried oregano

2 x 20-ounce cans of jackfruit

6 cups of homemade low-sodium vegetable broth

8 cloves of garlic (minced)

Pepper

Pinch of salt

Instructions:

- Set the Instant Pot on Sauté mode. Pour in the coconut oil.
- When it gets hot, add the onion and cook for 4 minutes. Then add garlic and cook for 1 minute.
- While stirring, add the coconut flour, cumin, red chile powder, oregano, pepper, and salt. Cook for 3 minutes. While stirring, add 2 cups of vegetable broth, cauliflower florets, and jackfruit.
- Use a potato masher to break apart the cauliflower florets and jackfruit. Add the remaining vegetable broth.
- Close the lid and seal it. Set on Manual and cook for 10 minutes on high pressure.

- After it is cooked, release the pressure naturally. Take off the lid and stir properly.
- Scoop into bowls and serve.

Nutrition Information per Serving:

Carbohydrates: 39.3g

Dietary Fiber: 3.7g

Fat: 17.4g

Protein: 7.3g

Calories: 314

SWEET POTATO HUMMUS

Time: 23 minutes

Servings: 4

Ingredients:

¼ cup of freshly squeezed lemon juice

⅓ cup of organic tahini sauce

½ pound of sweet potatoes (peeled and chopped)

1½ cups of homemade low-sodium vegetable broth

2 cloves of garlic (minced)

2 tablespoons of coconut oil

Pepper

Pinch of salt

Instructions:

- Put the potatoes and vegetable broth into the Instant Pot.
- Close the lid and seal it. Set on Manual and cook for 20 minutes on high pressure.
- After it cooks, release the pressure naturally. Take off the lid and place the potatoes in a bowl.
- Put the sweet potatoes, ½ cup of the liquid from the pot, tahini sauce, coconut oil, lemon juice, garlic cloves, pepper, and salt in a food processor.
- Blend until you get a creamy and smooth mixture then stir. Add seasoning to taste.
- Put the mixture in a glass jar or covered bowl. Put in a fridge until it is time to serve.

Nutrition Information per Serving:

Carbohydrates: 20.4g

Dietary Fiber: 4.3g

Fat: 17.3g

Protein: 4.4g

Calories: 249

CAULIFLOWER TIKKA MASALA

Time: 10 minutes

Servings: 4

Ingredients:

½ cup of pumpkin puree

½ cup of organic low-sodium bone broth

½ cup of unsweetened non-dairy yogurt or unsweetened coconut cream

1 tablespoon of garam masala

1 teaspoon of organic chili powder

1 medium red onion (finely chopped)

1 teaspoon of organic ground turmeric

1 tablespoon of dried fenugreek leaves

1 1-inch fresh ginger (peeled and grated)

1 teaspoon of smoked or regular paprika

1 medium beet (peeled, peeled, and diced)

1 tablespoon of fresh parsley, finely chopped

1 large cauliflower head (chopped into florets)

2 tablespoons of non-dairy butter or ghee

4 garlic cloves (minced)

Garnish: Roasted cashews and finely chopped cilantro

Instructions:

- Set the Instant Pot on Sauté mode then put the ghee in the pot.
- When the ghee melts, add the onion and cook for 3 minutes. Add the garlic and grated ginger and cook for an additional 2 minutes. Add the fenugreek, chili powder, paprika, turmeric, parsley, and garam masala then cook for a minute, while stirring.
- Put the beet, bone broth, and pumpkin puree in a blender and blend until it gets a bit chunky. Empty the contents of the blender into the Instant Pot and stir the cauliflower in.
- Lock the lid and seal it. Set on Manual and cook for 2 minutes on high pressure.
- When it is cooked, let it sit for a minute then quick release the pressure. Take off the lid.

- Stir the cream in to mix. Scoop into bowls then use cilantro and roasted cashews to garnish it. Serve.

Nutrition Information per Serving:

Carbohydrates: 33.23g

Dietary Fiber: 11.96g

Fat: 8.3g

Protein: 13.4g

Calories: 243

APPETIZER AND SIDE DISH RECIPES

LEMON BOK CHOY

Time: 13 minutes

Servings: 4

Ingredients:

1 tablespoon of sesame oil

1 teaspoon of freshly grated ginger

1 pound of baby bok choy (trimmed and sliced in half)

2 tablespoons of olive oil

2 tablespoons of low-sodium coconut aminos

4 garlic cloves (minced)

Juice and zest from 1 medium lemon

Pinch crushed red pepper flakes

Pinch of sea salt

Pepper

Instructions:

- Set the Instant Pot on Sauté mode and pour in the olive oil.
- When it gets hot, add the ginger and garlic then cook for 2 minutes.
- Stir in the lemon juice, coconut aminos, sesame oil, and lemon zest.
- Add the bok choy and stir well to coat. Cook for 4 minutes until the bok choy wilts.
- Use pepper, salt and red pepper flakes to season.

- Place on a platter and serve.

Nutrition Information per Serving:

Carbohydrates: 2.3g

Dietary Fiber: 0.3g

Fat: 7.93g

Protein: 1.82g

Calories: 76

CAULIFLOWER AND SWEET POTATO SALAD

Time: 15 minutes

Servings: 8

Ingredients:

½ pound of cauliflower florets (chopped)

½ cup of homemade Lectin-free mayonnaise

1 cup of water

1 tablespoon of organic Dijon mustard

1 tablespoon of fresh parsley (chopped)

1½ pounds of sweet potatoes (peeled and cubed)

2 large eggs

3 green onions (diced)

6 slices of bacon (chopped)

Pepper

Pinch of salt

Instructions:

- Pour a cup of water into the Instant Pot. Place a steamer basket in the pot.
- Place 2 large eggs, sweet potatoes, and cauliflower on the basket.
- Close the lid and seal it. Set on Manual and cook for 4 minutes on high pressure.
- Quick release the pressure when it is done. Take the lid off.
- Put the cauliflower and potatoes in a large bowl. Peel the eggs and dice them. Refrigerate the ingredients.
- Take out the steamer rack and pour away the water.
- Set the Instant Pot on Sauté mode and cook the bacon until they are browned. Turn the pot off. Refrigerate the bacon with the other ingredients. Allow to cool down for thirty minutes.
- Place the potatoes, bacon, cauliflower, and diced egg in a large bowl. Stir in the Dijon mustard, homemade mayonnaise, parsley, green onions, salt, and black pepper. Then serve.

Nutrition Information per Serving:

Carbohydrates: 29.1g

Dietary Fiber: 4.3g

Fat: 12.2g

Protein: 8.6g

Calories: 259

STEAMED ASPARAGUS

Time: 5 minutes

Servings: 4

Ingredients:

1 cup of water

1 pound of fresh asparagus (washed, woodsy end cut off)

Pepper

Pinch of salt

Instructions:

- Pour the water into the Instant Pot and place a steamer rack on the pot.
- Put the asparagus in a bowl. Lightly drizzle oil on it then use pepper and salt to season.
- Place the asparagus on the steamer rack.
- Close the lid and seal it. Set on Manual and cook for 2 minutes on high pressure.
- When it is done, either do a quick release or a natural release of the pressure. Then take off the lid.
- Take the steamer rack out of the pot. Place the asparagus on a platter and serve.

Nutrition Information per Serving:

Carbohydrates: 4.4g

Dietary Fiber: 2.4g

Fat: 0.1g

Protein: 2.5g

Calories. 23

BALSAMIC BRUSSEL SPROUTS

Time: 23 minutes

Servings: 4

Ingredients:

1 pound of fresh organic Brussel sprouts (trimmed and halved)

2 cups of water

2 tablespoons of balsamic vinegar

4 tablespoons of fresh chives (finely chopped)

6 slices of bacon (chopped)

Pepper

Pinch of salt

Instructions:

- Pour water into the Instant Pot and place a steamer basket on it.
- Place the Brussel sprouts on the basket.
- Close the lid and seal it. Set on Manual and cook for 2 minutes on high pressure.
- Quick release the pressure when it is done. Take off the lid.
- Place the Brussel sprouts in a bowl. Take out the steamer basket and get rid of the water.
- Set on Sauté mode and put the chopped bacon in the pot. Cook until it gets browned.
- Put the Brussel sprouts and bacon into the pot while the pot is still hot. Stir in the balsamic vinegar, pepper and salt.
- Place on a platter and use fresh chives to garnish. Serve.

Nutrition Information per Serving:

Carbohydrates: 10.9g

Dietary Fiber: 4.3g

Fat: 12.3g

Protein: 14.5g

Calories: 206

SOUTHERN-STYLE CABBAGE

Time: 9 minutes

Servings: 8

Ingredients:

¼ cup of non-dairy butter or ghee

1 large head of fresh green cabbage (cored and chopped)

2 cups of homemade low-sodium chicken broth

8 to 12 slices bacon (chopped)

Pinch of salt

Pepper

Instructions:

- Set the Instant Pot on Sauté mode. Place the bacon in the pot and cook until it is browned.

- Melt the non-dairy butter or ghee in the pot.
- Stir in the chicken broth, cabbage, black pepper, and salt.
- Close the lid and seal it. Set on Manual and cook for 3 minutes on high pressure.
- After cooking, quick release the pressure and take off the lid.
- Place the cabbage on a serving platter. Let it cool a little before serving.

Nutrition Information per Serving:

Carbohydrates: 9.5g

Dietary Fiber: 3.9g

Fat: 18.5g

Protein: 12.6g

Calories: 249

LEMON AND GARLIC BROCCOLI

Time: 23 minutes

Servings: 4

Ingredients:

1 cup of water

1 large garlic head

2 tablespoons of fresh lemon juice

2 tablespoons + 1 teaspoon of melted coconut oil

6 cups of fresh broccoli florets

Pepper

Pinch of crushed red pepper flakes

Pinch of salt

Instructions:

- Pour a cup of water into the Instant Pot. Then place a steamer rack in the pot.
- Place the garlic head in the skin on the rack. Drizzle the melted coconut oil over the garlic head.
- Close the lid and seal it. Set on Manual and cook for 7 minutes on high pressure.
- After cooking, release the pressure naturally for 10 minutes. Quick release the remaining pressure and take off the lid.
- Get the garlic off the rack. Squeeze out the skin from the garlic. Keep the broccoli on the rack.
- Close the lid and seal it. Set on Manual and cook for 10 minutes on high pressure.
- After cooking, quick release the pressure and take off the lid.
- Put the cooked garlic cloves, 2 tablespoons of coconut oil, lemon juice, red pepper flakes, pepper, and salt in a blender. Blend until it reaches a smooth consistency. Place the broccoli on a platter.
- Pour the sauce on the broccoli and serve.

Nutrition Information per Serving:

Carbohydrates: 16.3g

Dietary Fiber: 4.9g

Fat: 6.3g

Protein: 8.3g

Calories: 153

ASIAN BOK CHOY

Time: 16 minutes

Servings: 6

Ingredients:

1 teaspoon of sesame oil

1 pound of baby bok choy (trimmed)

1-inch of fresh ginger (peeled and minced)

1 tablespoon of low-sodium coconut aminos

1 tablespoon of Chinese seasoned rice vinegar

1 cup of homemade low-sodium vegetable broth

2 tablespoons of olive oil

2 cloves of garlic (minced)

Pepper

Pinch of salt

Instructions:

- Set the Instant Pot on Sauté mode and pour in the olive oil.
- When it gets hot, sauté the garlic cloves and ginger for 2 minutes.
- Add the baby bok choy and cook until it wilts a little.
- Add the vegetable broth and stir.
- Close the lid and seal it. Set on Manual and cook for 5 minutes on high pressure.
- After cooking, quick release the pressure. Take off the lid.
- Drizzle in the sesame oil, Chinese rice vinegar, and coconut aminos. Use pepper and salt to season.
- Place in a bowl and serve.

Nutrition Information per Serving:

Carbohydrates: 1.84g

Dietary Fiber: 0.2g

Fat: 4.86g

Protein: 2.06g

Calories: 68

LEMON BUTTER BRUSSEL SPROUTS

Time: 14 minutes

Servings: 4

Ingredients:

1 cup of water

1 pound of fresh Brussel sprouts (trimmed and halved)

4 tablespoons of non-dairy butter or ghee (melted)

Juice and zest from 1 medium lemon

Instructions:

- Pour a cup of water into the Instant Pot then place a steamer basket in it.
- Place the Brussel sprouts on the basket.
- Close the lid and seal it. Set on Manual and cook for 2 minutes on high pressure.
- Quick release the pressure when it is cooked. Take off the lid.
- Take the steamer basket and Brussel sprouts out of the pot. Pour out the water.

- Set the Instant Pot on Manual then put non-dairy butter or ghee in it. Add the lemon juice and zest when it melts. Then place the Brussel sprouts back into the pot. Allow simmering for 5 minutes until the fork gets tender.
- Place on a platter and serve.

Nutrition Information per Serving:

Carbohydrates: 11.7g

Dietary Fiber: 4.7g

Fat: 13.2g

Protein: 4.1g

Calories: 165

GINGER CARROTS

Time: 10 minutes

Servings: 10

Ingredients:

1 teaspoon of sea salt

1 cup of fresh orange juice

1 teaspoon of organic ground ginger

1 teaspoon of organic ground cinnamon

1 tablespoon of freshly squeezed lemon juice

2 pounds of fresh organic baby carrots

4 tablespoons of non-dairy butter or ghee (melted)

Instructions:

- Put all the ingredients into the Instant Pot. Stir properly to mix.
- Close the lid and seal it. Set on Manual and cook for 3 minutes on high pressure.
- After cooking, quick release the pressure. Take off the lid.
- Move the carrots to a serving dish.
- Set the Instant Pot on Sauté mode. Let the sauce simmer until it gets thicker.
- Scoop the sauce on the carrots then serve.

Nutrition Information per Serving:

Carbohydrates: 11.5g

Dietary Fiber: 2.3g

Fat: 5.2g

Protein: 0.9g

Calories: 95

CINNAMON BABY CARROTS

Time: 8 minutes

Servings: 8

Ingredients:

½ cup of water

½ teaspoon of organic pure vanilla extract

1 teaspoon of salt

2 pounds of fresh organic baby carrots

2 teaspoons of organic ground cinnamon powder

2 tablespoons of non-dairy butter or ghee (melted)

Instructions:

- Pour the water into the Instant Pot. Place the steamer basket in the pot.
- Place the carrots in the basket and season to taste with salt.
- Close the lid and seal it. Set on Manual and cook for 2 minutes on high pressure.
- When it is done, quick release the pressure. Take off the lid.
- Take out the steamer basket. Throw away the water. Put the carrots back into the pot.
- Stir in the melted ghee, cinnamon powder, and vanilla extract while the pot is still hot.
- Move to a platter and serve.

Nutrition Information per Serving:

Carbohydrates: 11.2g

Dietary Fiber: 2.8g

Fat: 2.9g

Protein: 1g

Calories: 73

DESSERT RECIPES

ORANGE ESSENTIAL OIL CHEESECAKE

Time: 33 minutes

Servings: 6

Crust Ingredients:

1½ cup of coconut flour, grounded mixed nuts, or almond flour

2 tablespoons of stevia or Swerve sweetener

3 tablespoons of coconut oil or ghee (melted)

Orange Cheesecake Filling Ingredients:

1 teaspoon of lime zest

1 teaspoon of orange essential oil

1 tablespoon of arrowroot powder

1 tablespoon of coconut oil, melted

1 cup of unsweetened coconut cream

2 cups of raw cashews

4 tablespoons of freshly squeezed orange juice

Instructions:

- Put all the crust ingredients into a bowl. Use your hands to mix them shortly.
- Press the crust into the springform pan of an Instant Pot.
- Heat the oven to 350oF and bake for about 10 minutes.
- Put the orange cheesecake filling ingredients in a blender and blend until really smooth.

169

- Pour the filling into the crusted springform pan then use foil to cover it.
- Pour 2 cups of water into the Instant Pot then place a trivet in the pot. Place the springform pan on the trivet.
- Close the lid and seal it. Set the Instant Pot on Manual and cook for 25 minutes on high pressure.
- After cooking, release the pressure naturally. Take off the lid.
- Move the pan to a cooling rack. Cool at room temperature for 1 hour. Place in a refrigerator to chill for 4 hours. Use non-dairy cream and fresh berries as toppings. Serve.

Nutrition Information per Serving:

Carbohydrates: 31g

Dietary Fiber: 4g

Fat: 48g

Protein: 12.3g

Calories: 456

LAVENDER CRÈME BRULEE

Time: 13 minutes

Servings: 4

Ingredients:

⅓ cup of swerve sweetener

1 teaspoon of pure vanilla extract

1 tablespoon of dried culinary lavender

1½ cups of water

2 cups of unsweetened coconut cream

8 egg yolk

Instructions:

- Put the sweetener and coconut cream in a bowl and stir properly to combine.
- Whisk in the egg yolks. Then stir in the lavender and vanilla extract.
- Use nonstick spray to grease the ramekins. Evenly divide the batter between the ramekins.
- Pour the water into the Instant Pot and place a trivet in the pot. Place the ramekins on the trivet.
- Lock the lid and seal it. Set on Manual and cook for 9 minutes on high pressure.
- After cooking, release the pressure naturally and take the lid off.
- Place the ramekins on a cool rack. Let it cool at room temperature for an hour. Place in a refrigerator to chill for 4 hours. Serve with the fresh berries.

Nutrition Information per Serving:

Carbohydrates: 13g

Dietary Fiber: 2g

Fat: 36.3g

Protein: 4.3g

Calories: 382

SWEET POTATO CHOCOLATE CAKE

Time: 1 hour

Servings: 14

Ingredients:

¾ cup of unsweetened coconut milk

¼ cup of erythritol sweetener or swerve

½ cup of nut butter

½ cup of coconut oil

½ teaspoon of baking soda

½ cup of coconut oil (melted)

½ cup of organic coconut flour

½ cup of organic cocoa powder

½ cup of chocolate protein powder

1 cup of mashed sweet potato

1 tablespoon of baking powder

Chocolate Frosting:

½ cup of cocoa powder

1 tablespoon of arrowroot powder

1 cup of unsweetened homemade applesauce

3 tablespoons of swerve sweetener

Instructions:

- Put the coconut flour, protein powder, cocoa powder, baking powder, and baking soda together in a large bowl and whisk properly.

- Get another bowl and put the sweet potato, nut butter, coconut oil, and coconut milk in it. Stir properly.
- Get a 7-inch cake pan to fit into the Instant Pot and grease it with non-stick spray.
- Pour the batter into the pan and use the foil to cover it.
- Pour 2 cups of water into the Instant Pot then place the trivet in the pot. Put the cake pan on the trivet.
- Close with the lid and seal it. Set on Manual and cook for 40 minutes on high pressure.
- Afterward, release the pressure naturally. Take off the lid.
- Put all the ingredients for the frosting into a large bowl. Stir properly. Put in a fridge to cool for 20 minutes.
- Take the cake out of the Instant Pot. Let it cool well.
- Spread the frosting of the chocolate on the cake. Serve.

Nutrition Information per Serving:

Carbohydrates: 15g

Dietary Fiber: 6g

Fat: 22g

Protein: 4g

Calories: 263

PEPPERMINT CHEESECAKE

Time: 40 minutes + 4 hours of refrigerating time

Servings: 6

Ingredients:

¼ cup of sour cream

½ cup of erythritol sweetener or swerve

½ teaspoons of pure peppermint extract

1 tablespoon of coconut

1½ teaspoons of pure vanilla extract

2 large organic eggs

2 cups of organic cream cheese (softened)

Pinch of salt

Chocolate Ganache:

⅓ cup of organic heavy cream

6-ounces of unsweetened chocolate chips (melted)

Pinch of salt

Crust:

1 cup of almond flour

2 tablespoons of swerve or erythritol sweetener

2 tablespoons of goat butter or ghee (melted)

Instructions:

- Press all the crust ingredients together in a springform pan that fits into the Instant Pot. Refrigerate for 10 minutes.
- Combine all the ingredients for the filling in a blender or large bowl. Stir properly.
- Pour the cheesecake filling into the springform pan. Use aluminum foil to cover it.
- Pour a cup of water into the Instant Pot and place a trivet inside. Place the pan on the trivet.
- Close the lid and seal it. Set on Manual and cook for 35 minutes on high pressure.

- After cooking, release the pressure naturally for 15 minutes. Quick release any pressure left and take off the lid.
- Take the pan out of the pot. Place on the counter to cool for 30 minutes. Chill in the fridge for 4 hours.
- Get a bowl and put the chocolate ganache ingredients in it. Mix properly then microwave for 30 seconds. Stir until it gets smoother.
- Place cheesecake on the platter. Drizzle the ganache over it. Serve.

Nutrition Information per Serving:

Carbohydrates: 30g

Dietary Fiber: 0.8g

Fat: 33.3g

Protein: 9g

Calories: 453

CHOCOLATE AVOCADO MUFFIN BITES

Time: 15 minutes

Servings: 6

Ingredients:

⅓ cup of unsweetened dark chocolate chips

½ teaspoon of baking soda

½ cup of coconut oil (melted)

½ teaspoon of baking powder

1 cup of apple juice

1 cup of coconut flour

1 teaspoon of organic cinnamon powder

1 cup of ripe avocados (peeled, pit removed, and mashed)

2 large organic eggs

2 teaspoons of organic vanilla extract

3 tablespoons of organic cocoa powder

Pinch of salt

Instructions:

- Put all the ingredients in a large bowl. Stir properly to mix.
- Use non-stick cooking spray to grease the silicone muffin cups or ramekins. Fill each with the mixture from the bowl.
- Pour a cup of water into the Instant Pot. Place the trivet in the pot.
- Place the muffin cups or ramekins on the trivet.
- Lock the lid and seal it. Set the pot on Manual and cook for 8 minutes on high pressure.
- After it is cooked, release the pressure naturally. Take off the lid.
- Place on a wire rack to cool down. Serve.

Nutrition Information per Serving:

Carbohydrates: 10g

Dietary Fiber: 3g

Fat: 25g

Protein: 4g

Calories: 272

ALMOND BUTTER CHOCOLATE CAKE

Time: 8 minutes

Servings: 1

Ingredients:

½ teaspoon of pure vanilla extract

1 large organic egg

1 teaspoon of ghee (melted)

1 tablespoon of almond butter (melted)

1 tablespoon of unsweetened coconut cream

2 tablespoons of cocoa powder

2 tablespoons of swerve sweetener

Instructions:

- Get a large bowl and put all the ingredients, apart from the almond butter, in it. Stir properly to combine.
- Use a non-stick spray to grease a ramekin. Pour the batter into the ramekin.
- Pour a cup of water into the Instant Pot. Place a trivet in the pot, then place the ramekin on it.
- Lock the lid and seal it. Set on Manual and cook for 2 minutes on high pressure.
- After cooking, quick release the pressure then take off the lid.
- Drizzle the melted almond butter on the cake of ramekin. Serve.

Nutrition Information per Serving:

Carbohydrates: 20.1g

Dietary Fiber: 5.2g

Fat: 22.6g

Protein: 11.2g

Calories: 257

APPLE CAKE

Time: 1 hour

Servings: 6

Ingredients:

¼ cup of coconut oil

¼ teaspoon of ground nutmeg

¼ cup of ghee or goat butter (melted)

½ cup of homemade applesauce

½ teaspoon of pure vanilla extract

½ cup of almonds (roughly chopped)

½ cup of erythritol sweetener or swerve

1 teaspoon of ground cinnamon powder

1½ cups of almond flour

2 large eggs

2 cups of fresh red or green apples (peeled, cored, and chopped)

Pinch of salt

Instructions:

- Get a large bowl and put all the ingredients, apart from the almonds, in it. Stir properly to combine.
- Use non-stick spray to grease a 7-inch cake pan to place in the Instant Pot.
- Pour the batter into the pan and use almonds as toppings. Use foil to cover the pan.
- Pour a cup of water into the Instant Pot. Place a trivet in the pot then place the cake pan on it.
- Close the lid and seal it. Set on Manual and cook for 60 minutes on high pressure.
- After cooking, release the pressure naturally. Take off the lid.
- Place the pan on a wire rack. Let it cool a little before you serve.

Nutrition Information per Serving:

Carbohydrates: 22g

Dietary Fiber: 3g

Fat: 27g

Protein: 5g

Calories: 313

MAPLE FLAN

Time: 1 hour and 30 minutes

Servings: 8

Ingredients:

½ teaspoon of salt

½ cup of maple syrup

1 tablespoon of pure vanilla extract

1½ cups of coconut milk

1½ cups of organic heavy cream

3 large organic eggs

Instructions:

- Get an Instant Pot souffle dish and put half of the maple syrup in it.
- Get a bowl and whisk the eggs in it along with a quarter cup of maple syrup.
- Get a medium saucepan and put the coconut milk, vanilla extract, heavy cream, and salt in it. Allow simmering for 5 minutes on low pressure.
- Temper the hot cream to the eggs; slowly drizzle a small part of the hot cream on the beaten eggs. Stir properly before adding the remaining hot cream. Constantly stir.
- Strain the ingredients into the souffle dish using a fine mesh strainer. Use aluminum foil to cover the dish.
- Pour 3 cups of water into the Instant Pot. Place the trivet in the pot and then place the souffle dish on the trivet.
- Lock the lid and seal it. Set on 'Slow Cook' and cook for 75 minutes on high pressure.
- When it is done, quick release the pressure. Take off the lid.
- Place the souffle dish on a wire rack. Let it cool for 60 minutes.
- Put in a fridge for 4 hours. Serve with the non-dairy cream and fresh berries.

Nutrition Information per Serving:

Carbohydrates: 18.63g

Dietary Fiber: 1.3g

Fat: 18g

Protein: 4.09g

Calories: 247

RASPBERRY CURD

Time: 8 minutes

Servings: 6

Ingredients:

½ teaspoon of lemon zest

1 tablespoon of fresh orange juice

1 cup of swerve or erythritol sweetener

2 egg yolks

2 cups of fresh raspberries

2 tablespoons of fresh lemon juice

2 tablespoons of coconut oil or ghee

Pinch of salt

Instructions:

- Put all the ingredients apart from the ghee and egg yolks into the Instant Pot. Stir properly.
- Lock the lid and seal it. Set on Manual and cook for 1 minute on high pressure.

- After cooking, release the pressure naturally for 5 minutes. Quick release any pressure left then take off the lid.
- Use an immersion blender to puree the raspberry mixture until it gets smooth.
- Set on Sauté mode. Stir the ghee and egg yolks into the raspberry mixture.
- Pour the raspberry mixture into a glass jar or covered bowl, then refrigerate.
- Serve over yogurt or non-dairy ice cream.

Nutrition Information per Serving:

Carbohydrates: 24.5g

Dietary Fiber: 3.2g

Fat: 1.8g

Protein: 1.63g

Calories: 115

STUFFED PEACHES

Time: 20 minutes

Servings: 6

Ingredients:

¼ cup of Swerve sweetener

¼ cup of organic almond flour or organic coconut flour

½ teaspoon of pure almond extract

1 teaspoon of organic ground cinnamon powder

2 tablespoons of coconut oil or ghee

6 organic fresh peaches (tops removed, pitted)

Pinch of salt

Instructions:

- Get a bowl and put the flour, cinnamon, swerve, almond extract, oil, and salt in it. Stir properly to combine.
- Evenly divide the mixture between the peaches.
- Pour a cup of water into the Instant Pot then place a steamer basket in it.
- Place the stuffed peaches on the steamer basket.
- Lock the lid and seal it. Set on Manual and cook for 3 minutes on high pressure.
- After cooking, quick release the pressure. Then take off the lid.
- Place the peaches on a platter. Use non-dairy ice cream to top. Then serve.

Nutrition Information per Serving:

Carbohydrates: 1.76g

Dietary Fiber: 0.9g

Fat: 14.21g

Protein: 9.11g

Calories: 172

4 WEEKS MEAL PLAN

WEEK 1

	Monday	Tuesday	Wednesday	Thursday	Friday	Saturday	Sunday
Breakfast	Breakfast Sausage and Cauliflower Mash	Hard Boiled Egg Loaf	Chorizo with Sweet Potato Hash	Turkey Sausage Frittata	Cauliflower Pudding	Egg Hash	Spinach and Mushroom Frittata
Lunch	Asian Bok Choy	Lamb Rogan	Cauliflower and Sweet Potato Salad	Balsamic Brussel Sprouts	Lemon Butter Brussel Sprouts	Lemon Bok Choy	Steamed Asparagus
Dinner	Chipotle Braised Lamb	Beef Curry	Spinach Sweet Potato Curry – Aloo Saag	Barbecue Jackfruit	Beef Burgundy with Mushrooms	Beef Meatballs with Mushroom Sauce	Wine and Coffee Beef Stew

WEEK 2

	Monday	Tuesday	Wednesday	Thursday	Friday	Saturday	Sunday
Breakfast	Egg Frittata with Asparagus	Spinach and Mushroom Frittata	Chorizo with Sweet Potato Hash	Hard Boiled Egg Loaf	Coconut Yogurt with Berries	Broccoli and Ham Frittata	Egg Hash
Lunch	Chicken Lime Avocado Soup	Chicken Kale Soup	Southern-Style Cabbage	Leek and Cauliflower Soup	Chicken Turmeric Soup	Chicken Paprikash	Hamburger Vegetable Soup
Dinner	Leg of Lamb with Mushroom Gravy	Adobo Pork	Pork Chops with Red Cabbage	Lamb Meatballs	Lemon Chicken	Creamy Chicken Thighs	Sloppy Joes

WEEK 3

	Monday	Tuesday	Wednesday	Thursday	Friday	Saturday	Sunday
Breakfast	Hard Boiled Egg Loaf	Egg Frittata with Asparagus	Breakfast Sausage and Cauliflower Mash	Egg Hash	Cauliflower Pudding	Turkey Sausage Frittata	Chorizo with Sweet Potato Hash
Lunch	Chicken Kale Soup	Chicken Lime Avocado Soup	Lemon Bok Choy	Lamb Rogan	Steamed Asparagus	Southern-Style Cabbage	Cauliflower and Sweet Potato Salad
Dinner	Wine and Coffee Beef Stew	Leg of Lamb with Mushroom Gravy	Beef Burgundy with Mushrooms	Adobo Pork	Creamy Chicken Thighs	Pork Chops with Red Cabbage	Spinach Sweet Potato Curry – Aloo Saag

WEEK 4

	Monday	Tuesday	Wednesday	Thursday	Friday	Saturday	Sunday
Breakfast	Turkey Sausage Frittata	Cauliflower Pudding	Chorizo with Sweet Potato Hash	Egg Hash	Broccoli and Ham Frittata	Breakfast Sausage and Cauliflower Mash	Egg Frittata with Asparagus
Lunch	Cauliflower and Sweet Potato Salad	Lamb Rogan	Chicken Kale Soup	Southern-Style Cabbage	Hamburger Vegetable Soup	Chicken Paprikash	Chicken Lime Avocado Soup
Dinner	Beef Burgundy with Mushrooms	Leg of Lamb with Mushroom Gravy	Chipotle Braised Lamb	Spinach Sweet Potato Curry – Aloo Saag	Lamb Meatballs	Pork Chops with Red Cabbage	Creamy Chicken Thighs

Manufactured by Amazon.ca
Acheson, AB

11830939R00103